READING/WRITING COMPANION

Mc
Graw
Hill
Education

Cover: Nathan Love, Erwin Madrid

mheducation.com/prek-12

Send all inquiries to:
McGraw-Hill Education
Two Penn Plaza
New York, NY 10121

ISBN: 978-0-07-901851-9
MHID: 0-07-901851-3

Printed in the United States of America.

8 9 LMN 25 24 23 22   C

Welcome to Wonders!

Read exciting **Literature**, **Science**, and **Social Studies** texts!

★ **LEARN** about the world around you!

★ **THINK**, **SPEAK**, and **WRITE** about genres!

★ **COLLABORATE** in discussion and inquiry!

★ **EXPRESS** yourself!

my.mheducation.com

Use your student login to read core texts, practice grammar and spelling, explore research projects and more!

GENRE STUDY 1 NARRATIVE NONFICTION

Essential Question 1
SHARED READ *"Room to Grow"* 2
Vocabulary/Compound Words 8
Ask and Answer Questions 10
Headings and Maps 11
Sequence 12
WRITING Respond to Reading 14
Research and Inquiry 15
ANCHOR TEXT Analyze *Gary the Dreamer* 16
WRITING Respond to Reading 19
PAIRED SELECTION Analyze *"Sharing Cultures"* 20
Author's Craft: Word Choice 23
Text Connections/Research and Inquiry 24
WRITING Personal Narrative 26

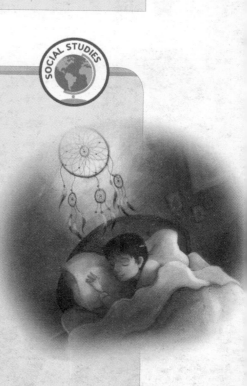

GENRE STUDY 2 REALISTIC FICTION

Essential Question 34
SHARED READ *"The Dream Catcher"* 36
Vocabulary/Context Clues 42
Visualize 44
Illustrations and Dialogue 45
Sequence 46
WRITING Respond to Reading 48
Research and Inquiry 49
ANCHOR TEXT Analyze *Yoon and the Jade Bracelet* 50
WRITING Respond to Reading 53
PAIRED SELECTION Analyze *"Family Traditions"* 54
Author's Craft: Voice 57
Text Connections/Research and Inquiry 58

GENRE STUDY 3 ARGUMENTATIVE TEXT

Essential Question..60

SHARED READ TIME FOR KIDS "Preserve and Protect"................62

Vocabulary/Multiple-Meaning Words.....................................66

Ask and Answer Questions..68

Captions, Maps, and Sidebars...69

Main Idea and Key Details...70

WRITING Respond to Reading..72

Research and Inquiry..73

ANCHOR TEXT Analyze *Protecting Our Parks*........................74

WRITING Respond to Reading..76

PAIRED SELECTION Analyze "5 Questions for George McDonald"...77

Author's Craft: Author's Purpose...79

Text Connections/Accuracy and Phrasing................................80

WRITING Argumentative Text..82

WRAP UP THE UNIT

SHOW WHAT YOU LEARNED

• Expository Text: "Remembering San Jacinto"........................90

• Realistic Fiction: "Sofia's Mexican Birthday"........................93

EXTEND YOUR LEARNING

• Comparing Genres..96

• Homographs..97

• Connect to Content..99

TRACK YOUR PROGRESS

• What Did You Learn?..100

Research and Inquiry..101

 Digital Tools Find this eBook and other resources at **my.mheducation.com**

UNIT 2

GENRE STUDY 1 EXPOSITORY TEXT

Essential Question 102
SHARED READ "Every Vote Counts!" 104
Vocabulary/Prefixes 110
Reread 112
Headings and Bar Graphs 113
Author's Point of View 114
WRITING Respond to Reading 116
Research and Inquiry 117
ANCHOR TEXT Analyze *Vote!* 118
WRITING Respond to Reading 121
PAIRED SELECTION Analyze "A Plan for the People" ... 122
Author's Craft: Author's Purpose 125
Text Connections/Research and Inquiry 126
WRITING Expository Essay 128

GENRE STUDY 2 HISTORICAL FICTION

Essential Question 136
SHARED READ "Sailing to America" 138
Vocabulary/Similes 144
Make Predictions 146
Events and Illustrations 147
Theme 148
WRITING Respond to Reading 150
Research and Inquiry 151
ANCHOR TEXT Analyze *The Castle on Hester Street* ... 152
WRITING Respond to Reading 155
PAIRED SELECTION Analyze "Next Stop, America!" ... 156
Author's Craft: Cause and Effect 159
Text Connections/Research and Inquiry 160

Richard Hutchings/Corbis Documentary/Getty Images

GENRE STUDY **3 POETRY**

Essential Question.. 162

SHARED READ "Empanada Day".. 164

Vocabulary/Simile... 168

Alliteration and Rhyme.. 170

Limerick and Free Verse... 171

Point of View.. 172

WRITING Respond to Reading... 174

Research and Inquiry.. 175

ANCHOR TEXT Analyze *The Inventor Thinks Up Helicopters*......... 176

WRITING Respond to Reading... 178

PAIRED SELECTION Analyze "Montgolfier Brothers' Hot Air Balloon" 179

Author's Craft: Voice.. 181

Text Connections/Expression and Phrasing.. 182

WRITING Poetry.. 184

WRAP UP THE UNIT

SHOW WHAT YOU LEARNED

• Expository Text: "Solving Local Problems"............................ 192

• Historical Fiction: "Welcome to America"............................... 195

EXTEND YOUR LEARNING

• Comparing Genres... 198

• Homographs.. 199

• Connect to Content... 200

TRACK YOUR PROGRESS

• What Did You Learn?... 202

Research and Inquiry.. 203

Digital Tools Find this eBook and other resources at **my.mheducation.com**

Talk About It

Essential Question

How do people from different
cultures contribute to a community?

David is sharing his culture at a Native American dance festival in his community. Learning about other cultures is important. Communities grow when people share their cultures.

Look at the photograph. What questions do you have about this? Talk with your partner about how David's community is learning about his culture. Write four ways in the word web.

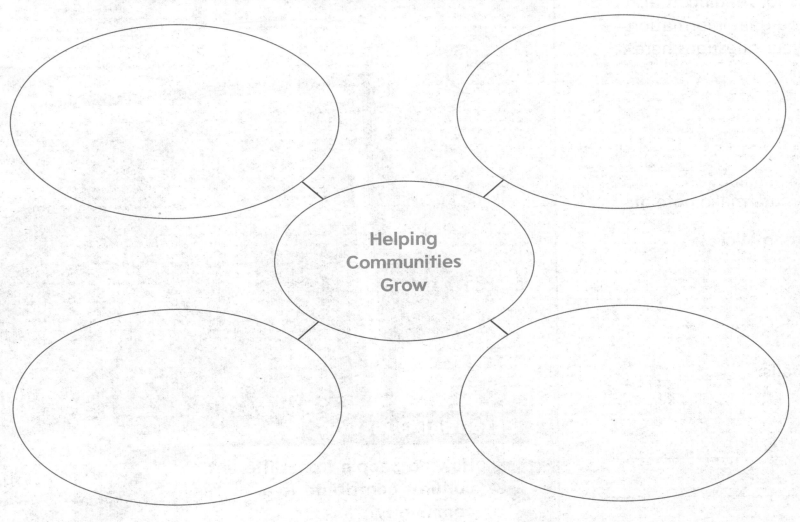

Helping Communities Grow

BLAST BACK! studysync

Go online to **my.mheducation.com** and read the "Who Made That?" Blast. Think about why learning about other cultures is important. Then blast back your response.

TAKE NOTES

Asking questions before you read helps you figure out your purpose for reading. It also helps you gain information. Write your questions here.

_____

_____

_____

As you read, make note of:

Interesting Words: _____

_____

_____

Key Details: _____

_____

_____

_____

_____

Room to Grow

Our new home in Portland

Essential Question

? **How do people from different cultures contribute to a community?**

Read how one family helps their community grow.

Spring in the City

My name is Kiku Sato. Last spring, my family and I moved from the country to the big city.

Our new home in Portland had no yard. There wasn't even a tiny plot of land. So Mama made an indoor garden. First she and Papa planted seeds in pots. Then they hung them from hooks. Next they crammed plants onto shelves. Green vines **tumbled** over desks. Soon our house had plants everywhere.

At first, I was **scared** to start school. I was afraid no one would be my friend. But I soon met a **classmate**. Jill Hernandez and I were **practicing** reading aloud one day. She helped me say her last name, and I helped her **pronounce** mine. The next day we were best friends. Jill spent lots of time at my house.

A map of Oregon

PENDLETON

PORTLAND

★ SALEM

OREGON

EUGENE

KEY
• CITY
★ CAPITAL
~ RIVER

ASHLAND

N
W E
S

NARRATIVE NONFICTION

FIND TEXT EVIDENCE 🔍

Read

Paragraph 2
Ask and Answer Questions
Why do Mama and Papa grow an indoor garden? **Circle** text evidence to answer.

Paragraph 3
Sequence
Underline what happens after Kiku meets Jill. What happens the next day?

_____

_____

Maps

Look at the map. **Draw a box around** where Kiku lives.

Reread

Author's Craft

Reread the first paragraph. How do you know who is telling the story?

An Idea for a Garden

One afternoon, Jill and her mother came to visit Mama and Papa and me. First they saw our beautiful potted plants. Jill's mother said, "Jill **admires** your indoor garden. She has told me so much about it."

We all sat down while Mama served tea. First she put green tea into the tea bowl. Then she added hot water and stirred. She handed the bowl to Jill's mother and bowed.

Mama's special tea bowls

Grandmother in Japan

"My mother taught me how to make tea," said Mama. "She also taught me how to plant a traditional Japanese garden. I learned to make the most of a small, compact space."

All of a sudden, Jill's mother smiled. "Can you help us with a project?" she asked. "Our **community** wants to plant a garden. Our plot is very small. There is so much we want to grow."

Papa looked at Mama, and they both bowed.

"Yes," they said.

(flowers) Japack/amanaimagesRF/Corbis; (bkgd) Wetzel and Company; (c) Margaret Lindmark

NARRATIVE NONFICTION

FIND TEXT EVIDENCE

Read

Paragraph 1
Ask and Answer Questions
Think of a question about Kiku's grandmother. Write it here.

_____

_____

_____

Underline text evidence that answers your question.

Paragraphs 2–3
Sequence
Circle what happens after Jill's mother asks Mama and Papa to help with the community garden project.

Paragraphs 2–4
Synthesize Information
Why does Jill's mother ask Kiku's mother for help? **Draw a box around** the text evidence.

FIND TEXT EVIDENCE

Read

Paragraph 1

Sequence

Underline two things that happen in order. Write the signal words that tell when they happen.

_____

_____

_____

Paragraph 2

Compound Words

Circle a compound word. Write what it means.

_____

_____

Reread

Author's Craft

Why is "A Garden Grows" a good heading for this section?

A Garden Grows

First we had a meeting with the community. Everyone agreed to **contribute**. Some people brought seeds, tools, and dirt. Then the next day we met and started our garden.

Papa built long, open boxes. Next, we filled them with dirt. The tallest box went close to the back wall. The boxes got shorter and shorter. The shortest box was in the front. "All the plants will get sunlight without making shade for the others," Mama said.

Papa builds boxes

Jill and I plant seeds

Then, we used round, flat stones to make a rock path. Papa said that in Japan, stones are an important part of a garden. Finally, we planted the seeds.

Jill and I worked in the garden all summer. Our community grew many **different** vegetables. At the end of the summer, we picked enough vegetables to have a cookout. Mama brought a big pot of miso and vegetable stew. Everyone thanked Mama and Papa for their help. They brought a bit of Japan to Portland. I was so **proud**.

Look what we picked!

Summarize

Use your notes and think about the sequence of events in "Room to Grow." Summarize the important events.

NARRATIVE NONFICTION

FIND TEXT EVIDENCE

> Read

Paragraph 1

Sequence

Underline what happens after Papa makes the rock path. Write the signal word here.

_____

Paragraph 2

Ask and Answer Questions

Write a question about the cookout.

_____

_____

> Reread

Author's Craft

How does the author help you understand how everyone feels about Mama and Papa?

Fluency

Take turns reading the last paragraph with expression.

Vocabulary

Use the sentences to talk with a partner about each word. Then answer the questions. Respond with your new vocabulary. It will help you remember the meaning of the words.

admires

My family **admires** my good test grades.

What do you admire about a friend?

_____

classmate

Don and his **classmate** Maria always eat lunch together.

What things do you do with a classmate?

_____

> **Build Your Word List** Reread the first paragraph on page 6. Draw a box around the word *meeting*. In your writer's notebook, use a Word web to write more forms of the word. Use a dictionary.

community

Many people in my **community** work together.

What do you like about your community?

_____

_____

contribute

Mom will **contribute** clothes to people who can use them.

What is something you can contribute?

_____

_____

practicing

Kyle has been **practicing** and now he can play lots of songs.

What skill can you improve by practicing?

_____

_____

pronounce

Cindy can **pronounce** her name in another language.

How can you learn how to pronounce new words?

_____

_____

scared

Our dog hides during storms because he is **scared**.

What do you do when you feel scared?

_____

_____

tumbled

The ripe tomatoes **tumbled** out of the big basket onto the ground.

What does tumbled mean?

_____

_____

Compound Words

A compound word is made up of two smaller words joined together. Use the meanings of the two smaller words to help you figure out what the compound word means.

🔍 **FIND TEXT EVIDENCE**

I see the compound word afternoon *on page 4. It has two smaller words,* after *and* noon. *I know what* after *means. I know* noon *means "12 o'clock." I think* afternoon *means "after 12 o'clock."*

One afternoon, Jill and her mother came to visit.

Your Turn Figure out the meaning of the compound word.

cookout, page 7 _____

_____

Ask and Answer Questions

Ask yourself questions as you read. Then look for details to support your answers.

🔍 **FIND TEXT EVIDENCE**
Look at the section "Spring in the City" on page 3. Think of a question and then read to answer it.

Quick Tip

Asking questions helps you understand the text better. As you read, stop and ask yourself questions. Then reread to find text evidence.

Page 3

Spring in the City

My name is Kiku Sato. Last spring, my family and I moved from the country to the big city.

Our new home in Portland had no yard. There wasn't even a tiny plot of land. So Mama made an indoor garden. First she and Papa planted seeds in pots. Then they hung them from hooks. Next they crammed plants onto shelves. Green vines **tumbled** over desks. Soon our house had plants everywhere.

I have a question. Why were there so many plants in Kiku's house? I read that they did not have a yard. So Mama and Papa planted lots of seeds. I can answer my question. Kiku's family liked to grow things and didn't have the space to do it outdoors.

Your Turn Reread the first paragraph on page 7. Think of one question. You might ask: *Why did Kiku's father use round, flat stones in the garden?* With a partner, reread the section to find text evidence. Then write the answer here.

_____

_____

Headings and Maps

"Room to Grow" is an **autobiography**. An autobiography

- is a kind of narrative nonfiction
- tells the true story of a person's life in order
- is written by that person and uses *I* and *me*
- may use text features such as headings and maps

FIND TEXT EVIDENCE

"Room to Grow" is an autobiography. It is a true story by Kiku about her life. She uses time-order words such as first, next, *and* finally. *She uses* I *and* me. *Kiku's story has headings and a map.*

Page 3

Spring in the City

My name is Kiku Sato. Last spring, my family and I moved from the country to the big city.

Our new home in Portland had no yard. There wasn't even a tiny plot of land. So Mama made an indoor garden. First she and Papa planted seeds in pots. Then they hung them from hooks. Next they crammed plants onto shelves. Green vines **tumbled** over desks. Soon our house had plants everywhere.

At first, I was **scared** to start school. I was afraid no one would be my friend. But I soon met a **classmate**. Jill Hernandez and I were **practicing** reading aloud one day. She helped me say her last name, and I helped her **pronounce** mine. The next day we were best friends. Jill spent lots of time at my house.

A map of Oregon

Readers to Writers

Look at the headings in each section of "Room to Grow." How do they help you understand the order of events?

When you write, think about how to use headings to organize your ideas.

Headings
A heading tells what a section of text is mostly about.

Map
A map is a flat drawing of a real place.

Your Turn Find parts of "Room to Grow" that tell you it is an autobiography. Tell your partner what you learned about Kiku and her culture. Write your answer below.

_____

_____

_____

Sequence

Sequence is the order in which important events take place. Look for words, such as *first, next, then,* and *finally.* These signal words show the sequence of events.

 FIND TEXT EVIDENCE

In this autobiography, the events are told in sequence. I see the signal word first *in "Spring in the City" on page 3. I will read to find out what happens next. I will look for signal words to help me.*

Quick Tip

Authors also use the sequence text structure to show steps in a process. Look for signal words that show the order of the steps.

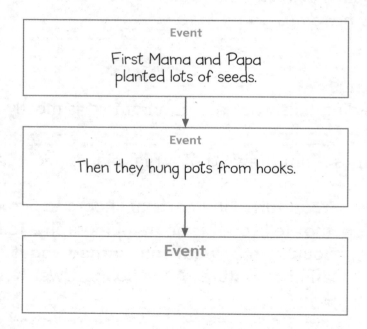

> **Event**
>
> First Mama and Papa planted lots of seeds.

↓

> **Event**
>
> Then they hung pots from hooks.

↓

> **Event**

 Your Turn Reread page 6. How do Kiku and her family help plant the garden? List the steps in order in your graphic organizer.

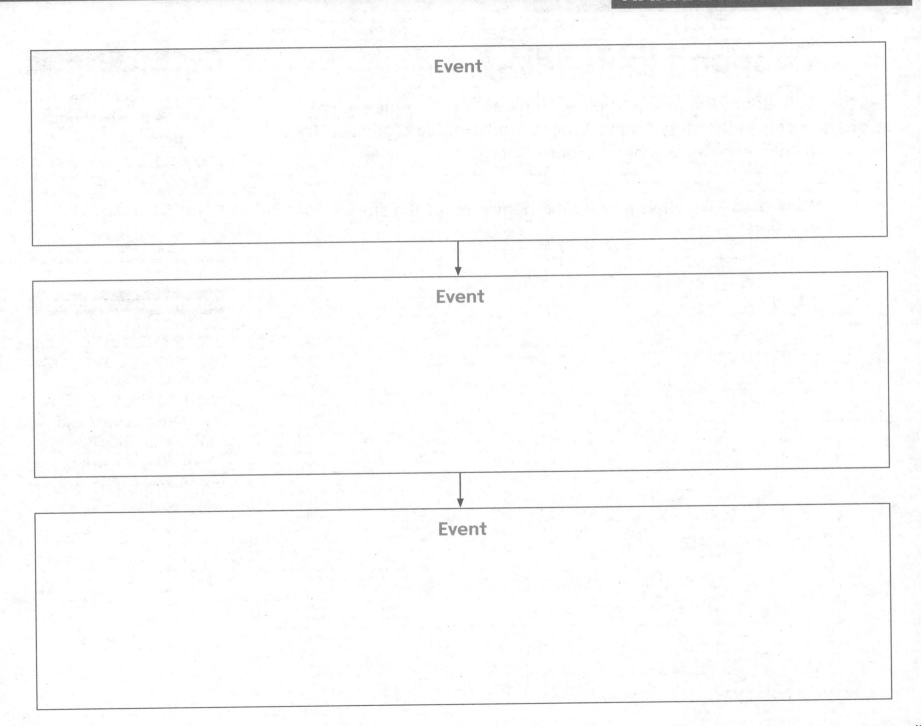

Event

Event

Event

Respond to Reading

COLLABORATE

Talk about the prompt below. Think about the sequence of events in the story. Use your notes and graphic organizer. Try to include new vocabulary in your response.

How does Kiku change from the beginning of the story to the end?

_____

_____

_____

_____

_____

_____

_____

_____

_____

_____

_____

_____

Quick Tip

Use these sentence starters to talk about the prompt.

At the beginning, Kiku was . . .

I read that she . . .

At the end, Kiku felt . . .

Grammar Connections

As you write your response, be sure to check that you have capitalized the names of people and the places they live. Remember to write complete sentences.

SOCIAL STUDIES

Using a Map

Most maps include features to help you understand them. A *compass rose* is a small drawing on a map that helps you find directions. The *map legend,* or *key,* tells you what the symbols on the map mean.

Look at the map. What is the state capital?

_____

Write the names of two cities.

_____

_____

COLLABORATE

Make a Map Choose a place in your community, like a park or school. Restate these steps aloud for your partner. Follow them to make a map.

1. Draw your map. Mark some interesting features, like a pond, picnic table, or grass.

2. Make a map legend with at least two symbols.

3. Draw a compass rose.

4. Share your map.

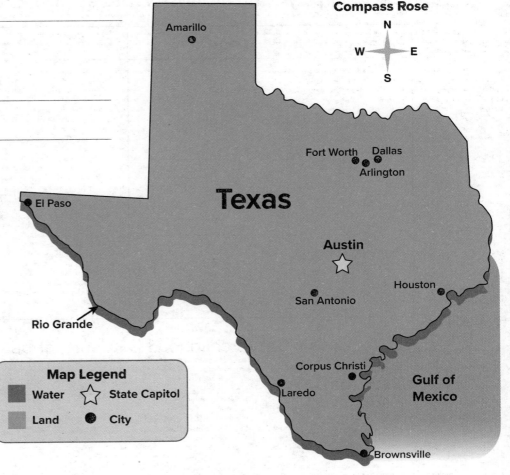

Compass Rose

N
W   E
S

Amarillo

Fort Worth   Dallas
Arlington

Texas

El Paso

Austin
☆

Houston

San Antonio

Rio Grande

Corpus Christi

Laredo

Gulf of Mexico

Brownsville

Map Legend
■ Water   ☆ State Capitol
■ Land   ● City

SHUTTERSTOCK

Gary the Dreamer

*Literature Anthology:
pages 10–21*

? **How is knowing what Gary did as a child important to understanding his autobiography?**

COLLABORATE

Talk About It Reread the first paragraph on page 13. Talk with a partner about how Gary played with his toys.

Cite Text Evidence What words and phrases help you picture how Gary plays with his toys? Write text evidence in the chart.

💡 **Make Inferences**

Use text evidence and what you know to make an inference. An inference is like a guess. What inference can you make about why Gary's childhood is important?

Text Evidence	What It Tells

Write I know Gary's childhood is important because it

shows that _____

_____

_____

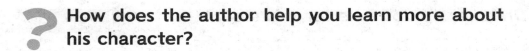

? **How does the author help you learn more about his character?**

COLLABORATE

Talk About It Look at pages 14 and 15. Turn and talk with a partner about what you see and what it tells you about Gary.

Cite Text Evidence How is Gary different from his classmates? Write text evidence and explain how you know.

Gary	His Classmates	How I Know

Write Gary Soto helps me know more about his life by _____

_____

_____

Quick Tip

I can use these sentence starters to talk about Gary.

I read that ...
I can use the
illustration to ...

Combine Information

Make a connection between what you already know and what you read about Gary Soto to create a new understanding. Talk about what Gary wants you to know and why.

Why is *Gary the Dreamer* a good title for this story?

 Talk About It Reread page 21. Talk about how Gary Soto uses the word *dreamed*.

Cite Text Evidence How does Gary use the word *dreamed* to show how he has changed? Write text evidence in the diagram.

 Make Inferences

Use Gary Soto's word choice to help you make an inference about the story's title. Make sure to use text evidence to support your ideas.

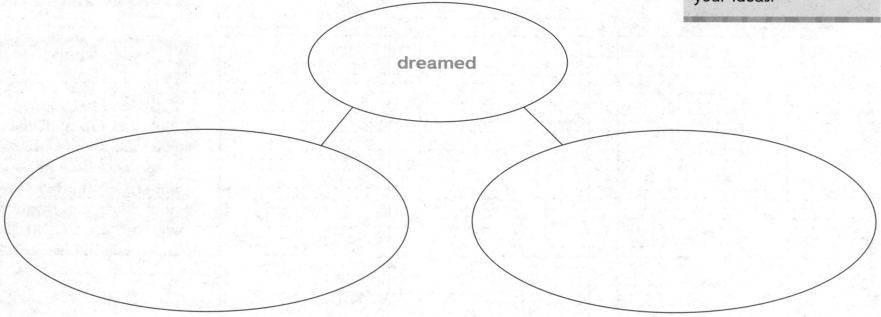

dreamed

Write *Gary the Dreamer* is a good title for this story because it

tells me that _____

_____

_____

Respond to Reading

COLLABORATE

Answer the prompt below. Think about how the author's use of words and phrases helps you visualize the events that he describes. Use your notes and graphic organizer.

How does Gary Soto help you see how his dreams helped him become a writer?

_____

_____

_____

_____

_____

_____

_____

_____

_____

_____

_____

Self-Selected Reading

Choose a text. Read the first two pages. If five or more words are unfamiliar, pick another text. Fill in your writer's notebook with the title, author, and genre and your purpose for reading the book.

Sharing Cultures

Literature Anthology:
pages 24–25

Pat Mora Loves Books

1   Pat Mora has a special word for how she feels about books. She calls it bookjoy. Born in El Paso, Texas in 1942, Pat learned to love books and reading from her mother. Books are magic to Pat.

2   "I wouldn't be me without books," she says.

3   Pat grew up in a bilingual home. That means she and her family spoke both English and Spanish. Pat is proud of her culture. She has written more than 36 children's books. Many of them are written in both English and Spanish.

4   Pat uses her stories and poems to share her culture. She works hard to share her love of books with children. Every year in April, many libraries and schools in America celebrate Día. Día is the nickname for Children's Day, Book Day. Día means "day" in Spanish. Children get together at libraries, schools, and parks to celebrate. It's like a big book *fiesta*, or party.

Reread and use the prompts to take notes in the text.

Reread paragraphs 1 and 2. How does the author help you understand how Pat Mora feels about books? **Underline** text evidence.

COLLABORATE

Reread paragraphs 3 and 4. Talk with a partner about how Pat Mora shares her culture with others. **Circle** text evidence.

Remember to take turns speaking when you work with a partner. Try to stay on topic. Speak clearly and pay attention to what your partner says.

Heroes and History

[5]   Kadir Nelson was born in Washington, DC, in 1974. When he was three years old, he picked up a pencil and started drawing. Then when he turned eleven, he spent the summer with his uncle. His uncle was an artist and teacher. Kadir says that summer changed his life.

[6]   Kadir is inspired by brave and honest leaders. He sometimes paints African American heroes he admires, such as Martin Luther King Jr. He also paints great athletes and everyday heroes, such as dads taking their children to the beach.

[7]   Kadir wants people to feel good when they look at his art. His paintings are colorful and real. They burst with action. Kadir says he has always been an artist. Sharing how he sees the world is part of who he is.

Reread paragraphs 5 and 6. How does the author help you understand how Kadir felt about spending the summer with his uncle?

_____

_____

Circle two details that support your answer.

Reread paragraph 7. How does the author help you visualize Kadir's paintings? **Underline** text evidence.

COLLABORATE

Turn and talk with a partner about the heading. Why is "Heroes and History" a good heading for this section? **Draw a box around** text evidence. Write your answer here.

_____

_____

_____

? **How does the author use words and phrases to help you visualize how people share their cultures?**

Talk About It Reread pages 20 and 21. Talk with a partner about how Pat Mora and Kadir Nelson share their cultures.

Cite Text Evidence What words and phrases help you picture how people share their cultures? Write three ways and how they help.

Text Evidence	How It Helps

Write I can visualize how people share their cultures because

_____

_____

Word Choice

Writers use strong, concrete words, and details to make their writing interesting and clear. Strong words show rather than tell.

🔍 **FIND TEXT EVIDENCE**

On page 24 in "Sharing Cultures," the author uses the word bilingual *to tell about Pat Mora's culture. By choosing this word, the author is helping you understand that Pat Mora grew up in a home where two languages were spoken.*

> Pat grew up in a bilingual home. That means she and her family spoke both English and Spanish.

Your Turn Reread paragraph 7 on page 21.

• What words and phrases does the author use to describe

Kadir's art? _____

_____

• How do these words help you picture what Kadir's art is like?

_____

_____

_____

If you want your readers to picture in their minds what you are writing about, choose words that are strong. A thesaurus can help you choose words that give a clear picture.

Text Connections

? **How is the reason why the artist painted this mural the same as why Gary Soto wrote *Gary the Dreamer*?**

Talk About It With a partner, talk about the people you see in the mural. Look closely at what each worker does and how the artist shows how they each feel.

Cite Text Evidence Read the caption. Then circle three people in the mural. Write what they do in the margin next to them. In the caption, underline clues that help you figure out why the artist painted his mural.

Write Connect how both the artist and Gary Soto

share their art and stories to share their love for

and pride for their cultures. _____

_____

_____

_____

The artist painted this mural on a building in Chicago, Illinois. He used real people. It celebrates the community's hardworking Latin American people.

Quick Tip

You can find clues in the mural that show how the people in this community feel. This will help you compare text to art.

Present Your Work

Decide how you will present your community map to the class. Create an online slide show or a digital poster. Use the checklist to help you improve your presentation.

Before I present, I will practice my presentation by

_____

I think my presentation was _____.

I know because _____

_____

_____

_____

✔ **Presenting Checklist**

☐ I will practice my presentation.

☐ I will look at the audience.

☐ I will speak clearly and slowly.

☐ I will make sure that everyone can see my map.

Literature Anthology: pages 10–21

Expert Model

Features of Personal Narrative

Personal narrative is a kind of narrative nonfiction. A personal narrative

- tells about a true story of a person's life in order
- shares the writer's feelings about an experience
- has a beginning, a middle, and end

Analyze an Expert Model Reread the last paragraph of *Gary the Dreamer* on page 11 in the **Literature Anthology**. Use text evidence to answer the questions.

How does Gary Soto make reading about his pets more

interesting? _____

_____

_____

What does the last sentence tell you about Gary? _____

_____

_____

Word Wise

Writers use pronouns, such as *I, we, she, he, him, her,* to take the place of nouns. For example, Gary Soto says "Once, when Boots came by, I tossed a piece of bark at *him*." The pronoun *him* stands for Boots. Pronouns can tell readers if the author is writing about themselves or someone else.

Plan: Choose Your Topic

Brainstorm With a partner, brainstorm memories of when you tried your hardest to do something. Use the sentence starters below to talk about your ideas.

I remember when . . .

This made me feel . . .

Writing Prompt Choose one of your memories to write about in a personal narrative.

I will write about _____

_____

Purpose and Audience An author's purpose is the main reason for writing. Your audience is who will be reading it.

Who will read your personal narrative? _____

_____

_____

Plan Think about what you want your readers to learn about you. Ask yourself questions and answer them in your writer's notebook.

Quick Tip

When you write a personal narrative, you are sharing your thoughts and feelings with your audience. As you plan your personal narrative, ask yourself: *What do I want people to remember about my story?*

Plan: Sequence

Sequence Writers tell stories in sequence, or the order that events happen. The sequence of events in a story helps readers understand what happens and why it happens.

Let's look at another expert model. Read this passage from "Room to Grow."

> First she and Papa planted seeds in pots. Then they hung them from hooks. Next they crammed plants onto shelves. Green vines tumbled over desks. Soon our house had plants everywhere.

Signal words show the sequence of events. Now reread the passage and **circle** four signal words.

Think about the memory you are going to write about. Talk with a partner about what you did. Use these sentence starters as you tell your story:

First, I . . .
Then, I . . .
Finally, I . . .

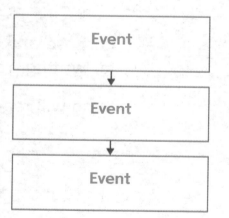

Event
Event
Event

Chart In your writer's notebook, draw a Sequence chart. Fill in the chart to plan your writing. Be sure to add signal words.

Draft

Descriptive Details Authors use descriptive details to help readers see, hear, and feel what they are describing. Read the first paragraph of *Gary the Dreamer* on page 21 in the **Literature Anthology**. Use text evidence to answer the questions below.

How does Gary Soto describe the sound of the water?

_____

_____

What does he think the bubbles look like?

_____

_____

Think about putting bubbles on your face to make a beard. Write two words that describe how the bubbles might feel.

_____

_____

Write a Draft Look over the Sequence chart that you made. Use it to help you write your draft in your writer's notebook. Remember to use signal words and descriptive details.

Quick Tip

When you write a **draft,** you are taking a first pass at your writing. You don't have to worry about making mistakes when you write a draft. There will be time to fix those mistakes in later stages. The important thing is to get all your ideas down on paper.

Revise

Sentence Fluency Writers use a variety of sentence types, such as statements, questions, and exclamations. Writers also vary the length of their sentences. This helps make their writing more interesting to read.

Reread page 18 of *Gary the Dreamer* in the **Literature Anthology**. Talk with a partner about how the author uses different kinds of sentences. Write about it here.

_____

_____

_____

Revise It's time to revise your writing. Read your draft and look for places where you might

- vary the lengths of your sentences

- use different kinds of sentences

Circle two sentences from your draft that you can change. Revise and write them here.

1 _____

2 _____

_____

Peer Conferences

Review a Draft Listen carefully as a partner reads his or her draft aloud. Tell what you like about the draft. Use these sentence starters to help you discuss your partner's draft.

I like this part because it made me feel . . .

Can this sentence be . . .

Add another detail to describe . . .

Partner Feedback After you take turns giving each other feedback, write one of the suggestions from your partner that you will use in your revision.

_____

_____

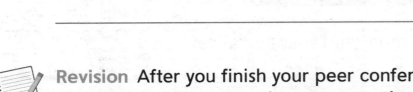

Revision After you finish your peer conference, use the Revising Checklist to help you make your narrative better. Remember to use the rubric on page 33 to help you with your revision.

Digital Tools

For more information about how to have peer conferences watch "Peer Conferencing." Go to **my.mheducation.com**.

✓ Revising Checklist

- ☐ Does my narrative have a logical sequence of events?
- ☐ Is there a beginning, middle, and end?
- ☐ Does my narrative include descriptive details?
- ☐ Did I use different kinds of sentences?

Edit and Proofread

After you revise your narrative, proofread it to find any mistakes in grammar, spelling, and punctuation. Read your draft at least three times. This will help you catch any mistakes. Use the checklist below to edit your sentences.

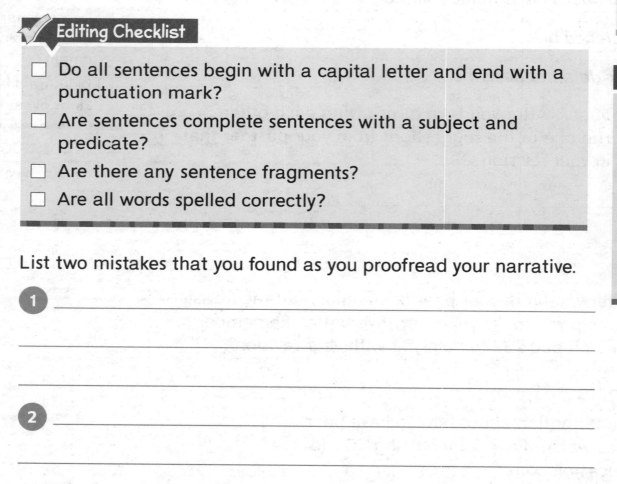

✓ Editing Checklist

- ☐ Do all sentences begin with a capital letter and end with a punctuation mark?
- ☐ Are sentences complete sentences with a subject and predicate?
- ☐ Are there any sentence fragments?
- ☐ Are all words spelled correctly?

List two mistakes that you found as you proofread your narrative.

1 _____

_____

_____

2 _____

_____

_____

Tech Tip

If you wrote your draft on a computer, print it out. It's easier to check for mistakes on paper than reading the text on a screen.

Grammar Connections

When you proofread your draft for punctuation mistakes, remember that you should always capitalize the pronoun *I* as in, "At lunch, I ate pizza and carrot sticks."

Publish, Present, and Evaluate

Publishing When you publish your writing, you create a neat final copy that is free of mistakes. If you are not using a computer, use your best handwriting. Write legibly in print or cursive.

Presentation When you are ready to present, practice your presentation. Use the presenting checklist.

Evaluate After you publish, use the rubric to evaluate it.

<table>
<tr><td>✓ **Presenting Checklist**</td></tr>
<tr><td>☐ Look at the audience.</td></tr>
<tr><td>☐ Speak slowly and clearly.</td></tr>
<tr><td>☐ Speak loudly enough so that everyone can hear you.</td></tr>
<tr><td>☐ Answer questions thoughtfully.</td></tr>
</table>

What did you do successfully? _____

_____

What needs more work? _____

_____

4	3	2	1
• tells about a personal experience and includes thoughts and feelings • presents events in the correct order • uses a variety of sentences	• tells about a personal experience and includes some feelings • presents events in the correct order • varies sentences	• tells about a personal experience • includes events that are told out of order • uses only simple sentences	• does not tell about a personal experience • tells events out order and is confusing • sentences are choppy

Talk About It

Essential Question

What can traditions teach you about cultures?

I live in Alaska. My family and I share our Yupik traditions through dance. I am holding traditional Yupik dance fans. Traditions are passed down in families. They help us learn about our culture.

Look at the photograph. Talk about what the Yupik dancer is wearing and holding. Talk with your partner about how your family shares traditions. Write your ideas in the word web.

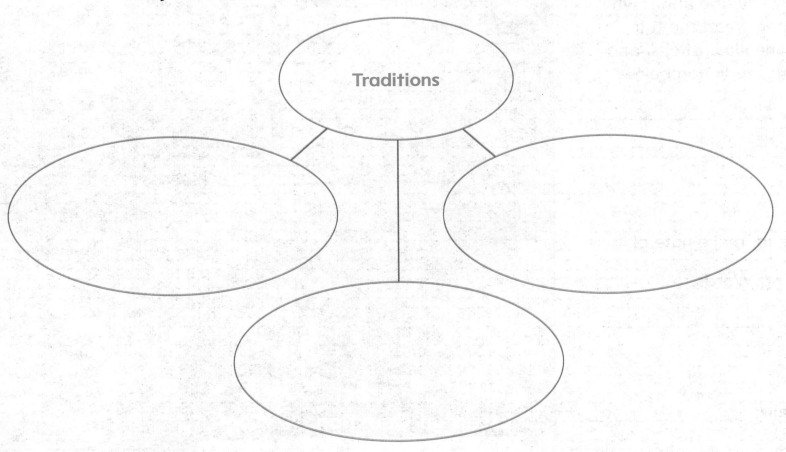

Traditions

Go online to **my.mheducation.com** and read "The Good Doctor" Blast. Think about what Dr. Hector P. Garcia Day can teach you about Texas history. Then blast back your response.

TAKE NOTES

To help yourself focus as you read, preview the text and make a prediction about what will happen. Read the title, preview the illustrations, and write your prediction below.

_____

_____

_____

As you read, make note of:

Interesting Words:

_____

_____

Key Details: _____

_____

_____

_____

_____

The Dream Catcher

Essential Question

? **What can traditions teach you about cultures?**

Read how Peter learns about his culture.

P eter walked home from school. Salty tears ran down his cheeks, and his stomach hurt. He didn't know what to do. Grandmother was waiting for him on the front porch.

"What's wrong, Biyen?" said Peter's grandmother. Biyen was Peter's Ojibwe name. He called his grandmother Nokomis.

Peter looked up. "I have to give a presentation where I talk about a family **tradition**. I know we have lots of beliefs and customs. Can you **remind** me of one?"

Nokomis smiled and nodded her head.

"Come with me," she said.

FIND TEXT EVIDENCE

Read

Paragraphs 1-2
Sequence
What happens after Peter gets home from school?

_____

_____

Circle text evidence that supports your answer.

Paragraphs 3–5
Dialogue
Underline why Peter is upset. What does he ask Nokomis?

_____

_____

Reread
Author's Craft

How does the author help you understand about Peter's culture?

FIND TEXT EVIDENCE

Read

Paragraphs 1–2

Dreamcatcher

Sequence

What does Nokomis do to help Peter with his problem?

_____

_____

_____

Circle text evidence.

Paragraph 3–4

Visualize

Underline details that help you picture what the dream catcher looks like.

Illustrations

Write one detail the illustration shows that isn't in the text.

_____

_____

_____

Peter followed Nokomis. She went to a closet and stretched to reach the top shelf. She pulled out a small box and blew away the dust. She handed it to Peter.

"Open it," she said.

Peter opened the box. He spotted a wooden hoop inside. It was in the shape of a circle. String was woven and twisted around the hoop. It looked like a spider web. A black bead sat near the center. Feathers hung from the bottom.

Peter wiped away his tears and smiled.

"This is a dream catcher," said Nokomis. "Our people have made these for many generations. Circles are **symbols** of strength. Let's hang it over your bed tonight. It will catch your bad dreams in the web, and your good dreams will fall through the center. Maybe it will give you **courage** to do your presentation."

"Can I take this one to school?" asked Peter.

"No, Biyen," said Nokomis. "This dream catcher is **precious**. I got it when I was your age, and it means a lot to me."

FIND TEXT EVIDENCE

Read

Paragraph 1
Dialogue
Circle what Nokomis says they will do with the dream catcher. **Write** what Nokomis tells Peter the dream catcher will do.

_____

_____

Paragraphs 2–3
Make Inferences
Why doesn't Nokomis want Peter to take her dream catcher to school?

_____

_____

Underline text evidence.

Reread
Author's Craft

How does the author help you understand that dream catchers are an Ojibwe tradition?

SHARED READ

FIND TEXT EVIDENCE

Read

Paragraphs 1–3
Dialogue

Draw a box around what Nokomis tells Peter they could do. How does Peter respond?

_____

_____

Paragraph 4
Context Clues

Circle the word that helps you figure out what *gazed* means.

Paragraph 5
Sequence

When does Peter tell Nokomis his plan?

_____

Underline text evidencce.

Reread

Author's Craft

How does the illustration help you understand how Peter feels about the dream catcher?

Peter felt **disappointment** because he wanted to share the dream catcher with his class.

"We could make you one," said Nokomis.

"I'd like that!" cried Peter.

Nokomis and Peter worked together and made a dream catcher. That night, as he gazed and looked at the dream catcher over his bed, he made a plan.

The next morning he told Nokomis his plan. "I'm going to show my class how to make a dream catcher," he said.

"That's a great idea!" said Nokomis. "Let's **celebrate** after your presentation. I will bake corn cookies and we will have a traditional Ojibwe party."

Peter shared his dream catcher with his classmates and showed them how to make their own. Peter didn't feel nervous or scared at all. He felt **pride** in his culture. He felt pride in himself, too.

Summarize

Use your notes and think about the sequence of events in "The Dream Catcher." Summarize the important events.

FIND TEXT EVIDENCE

Read

Paragraph 1
Dialogue
What does Nokomis think of Peter's plan? **Underline** what she says to Peter.

Paragraph 1
Visualize
Write something Nokomis and Peter will do at their party.

_____

_____

Circle text evidence.

Paragraph 2
Sequence
Draw a box around two things Peter does at school.

Reread

Author's Craft

How do you know how Peter feels after his presentation?

Vocabulary

Use the sentences to talk with a partner about each word. Then answer the questions.

celebrate

Kayla and her friends like to **celebrate** the Fourth of July together.

What do you like to celebrate?

_____

_____

courage

Firefighters show bravery and **courage**.

What word means the same as courage?

_____

_____

disappointment

Jason felt **disappointment** when his class trip was cancelled.

What would make you feel disappointment?

_____

_____

precious

This necklace is **precious** to my grandmother because her mother gave it to her.

Name something that is precious to you.

_____

_____

pride

I take **pride** in my drawings.

When do you feel pride?

_____

_____

Build Your Word List Pick one of the interesting words from your list on page 36. Use a thesaurus to look up the word. Write the word and two of its synonyms and antonyms in your writer's notebook.

remind

Mom will **remind** me to clean my room.

What is something someone needs to remind you to do?

_____

_____

symbols

The eagle and the flag are **symbols** of our country.

Name another symbol.

_____

_____

tradition

My family's Thanksgiving **tradition** is to cook dinner together.

Describe a tradition people share.

_____

_____

Context Clues

If you come across a word you don't know, use context clues. Look for other words in the same sentence that can help you figure out the unfamiliar word's meaning.

🔍 FIND TEXT EVIDENCE

I read this sentence on page 37. I'm not sure what the word presentation _means. I see the words_ talk about. _This clue helps me figure out what_ presentation _means. A presentation is a talk or speech._

I have to give a presentation where I talk about a family tradition.

Your Turn Use context clues to figure out the meaning of the word.

woven, page 38 _____

_____

Janet Broxon

Visualize

As you read, use details to visualize, or form pictures in your mind. This will help you better understand the text.

🔍 **FIND TEXT EVIDENCE**

How does Peter feel at the beginning of the story? Use the details in the first paragraph on page 37.

Page 37

Peter walked home from school. Salty tears ran down his cheeks, and his stomach hurt. He didn't know what to do. Grandmother was waiting for him on the front porch.

"What's wrong, Biyen?" said Peter's grandmother. Biyen was Peter's Ojibwe name. He called his grandmother Nokomis.

I can visualize how Peter feels at the beginning of the story. He walked home. Salty tears ran down his cheeks. His stomach hurt. These details help me figure out that Peter feels sad and upset.

Your Turn Reread page 38. How does Peter feel when he first sees the dream catcher? Take turns talking about what you visualize. Then use text evidence to answer the question.

_____

_____

_____

Illustrations and Dialogue

"The Dream Catcher" is **realistic fiction**. Realistic fiction

- is a made-up story that could really happen
- has a beginning, middle, and end
- has illustrations and dialogue

🔍 FIND TEXT EVIDENCE

"The Dream Catcher" is realistic fiction. I know because the events could really happen. It also has realistic illustrations and dialogue.

Page 37

Peter walked home from school. Salty tears ran down his cheeks, and his stomach hurt. He didn't know what to do. Grandmother was waiting for him on the front porch.

"What's wrong, Biyen?" said Peter's grandmother. Biyen was Peter's Ojibwe name. He called his grandmother Nokomis.

Peter looked up. "I have to give a presentation where I talk about a family **tradition**. I know we have lots of beliefs and customs. Can you **remind** me of one?"

Nokomis smiled and nodded her head.

"Come with me," she said.

Illustrations
Illustrations give more information or details about characters and setting.

Dialogue
Dialogue is what the characters say to one another.

COLLABORATE

Your Turn Tell your partner why "The Dream Catcher" is realistic fiction. Find two things in the story that could happen in real life. Write your answer below.

_____

_____

_____

Sequence

A character's actions make up the plot, or events, in a story. Plot events can be told in the order they happen. A plot always has a beginning, middle, and end.

🔍 FIND TEXT EVIDENCE

At the beginning of the story, I read to see what the characters say and do. Then I read on to see what happens in the middle of the story.

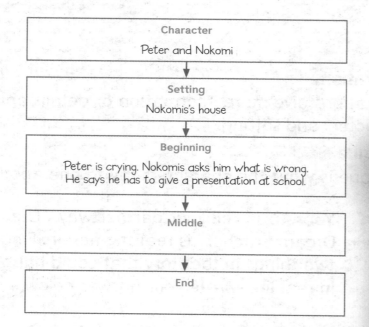

Character
Peter and Nokomi

Setting
Nokomis's house

Beginning
Peter is crying. Nokomis asks him what is wrong. He says he has to give a presentation at school.

Middle

End

COLLABORATE

Your Turn Reread pages 38–41. What happens in the middle and at the end of the story? List the events in order in your graphic organizer.

©Westend61/SuperStock

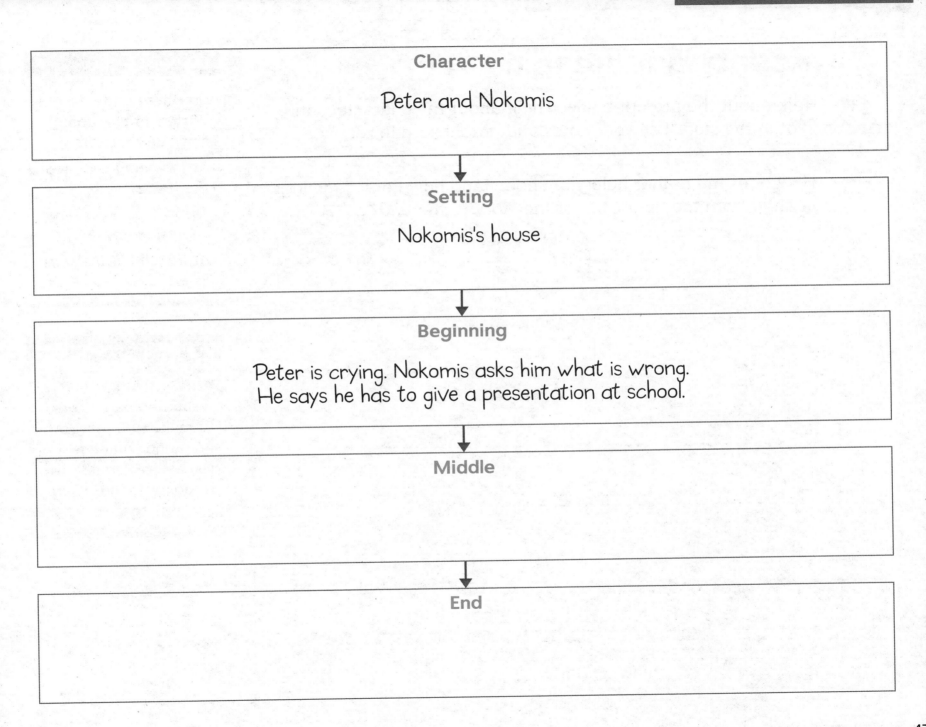

Character

Peter and Nokomis

Setting

Nokomis's house

Beginning

Peter is crying. Nokomis asks him what is wrong.
He says he has to give a presentation at school.

Middle

End

Respond to Reading

COLLABORATE

Talk about the prompt below. Think about the characters and plot in the story. Use your notes and graphic organizer.

How does the author help you understand how Peter's feelings change from the beginning of the story to the end?

_____

_____

_____

_____

_____

_____

_____

_____

Quick Tip

Use these sentence starters to talk about how Peter feels.

At the beginning I read that Peter…

The author helps me understand by…

At the end of the story, Peter…

Grammar Connections

After you write your response, read it over to make sure that you are using complete sentences. Reread your response to make sure it makes sense.

Generate Questions

Making a list of questions you have about a topic can help you figure out the best way to research it. There are two ways to do research:

- **Formal inquiry** means using encyclopedias, books, articles, and reliable websites.

- **Informal inquiry** means talking to people, asking questions, and observing to get information.

Write a question about a family tradition.

_____

Name a way you could find the answer through formal inquiry.

_____

Name a way you could find the answer through informal inquiry.

_____

Create a Culture Quilt Talk about one of your family traditions. Then use these steps to make a square for a class culture quilt.

1. Use formal and informal inquiry to research your tradition.

2. Write a paragraph about the tradition on a square of paper.

3. Draw a picture of the tradition on the other side of the square.

Fuse/Getty Images

Yoon and the Jade Bracelet

Literature Anthology: pages 26–43

 How does the author help you understand how Yoon feels about the present her mother gives her?

 Talk About It Reread page 28. Talk with a partner about what Yoon really wants for her birthday. How do you know?

Cite Text Evidence What words and phrases show how Yoon feels? Write text evidence here.

Text Evidence	How Yoon Feels

Make Inferences

An inference is a guess you make based on evidence. What inference can you make about why Yoon smiles even though she is disappointed?

Write The author helps me understand how Yoon feels about the

present by _____

_____

_____

How do you know jade is important in Yoon's culture?

Talk About It Reread the last paragraph on page 31. Talk about what Yoon's mother says about jade.

Cite Text Evidence What clues help you see that jade is important in Yoon's culture? Write text evidence in the chart.

Yoon's Mother Says	This Tells Me

Write I know that jade is important to Yoon's culture because

_____

_____

_____

_____

Quick Tip

I can use these sentence starters when we talk about jade.

Yoon's mother uses words like…

This helps me understand that jade is…

Evaluate Information

Think about the different things Yoon's mother says about jade. What do these different things have in common?

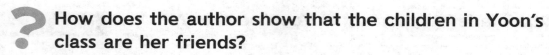

? **How does the author show that the children in Yoon's class are her friends?**

 Make Inferences

Talk About It Reread page 39. Talk with a partner about what Yoon's classmates do and say.

Cite Text Evidence What do Yoon's classmates do and say when their teacher asks about the bracelet? Write clues in the chart.

An inference is a guess based on text evidence. Use what you know to make an inference about how Yoon's classmates feel about her.

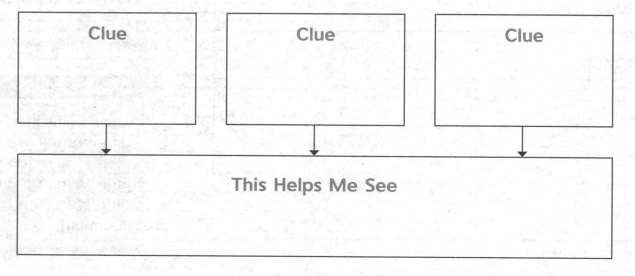

Clue	Clue	Clue

This Helps Me See

Write I know the children are Yoon's friends because the author

_____

_____

_____

_____

Respond to Reading

COLLABORATE

Answer the prompt below. Think about how the author helps you understand Yoon's feelings, thoughts, and actions throughout the story. Use your notes and graphic organizer.

Quick Tip

Use these sentence starters to talk about how Yoon changes.

At the beginning, Yoon wants…

The author helps me see that…

At the end, Yoon…

How does Yoon change from the beginning of the story to the end?

_____

_____

_____

_____

_____

_____

_____

_____

Self-Selected Reading

Choose a text. In your writer's notebook, write the title, author, and genre of the book. As you read, make a connection to ideas in other texts you have read or to a personal experience. Write your ideas in your writer's notebook.

Family Traditions

Celebrating a New Year

1   Chinese families celebrate Lunar New Year. Lunar New Year happens in January or February. It lasts about two weeks. The holiday means that winter is ending. Spring is on the way!

2   The traditions for Lunar New Year are very old. Adults give children bright red envelopes. Red stands for good luck and happiness. The envelopes are full of good luck money.

3   This holiday is also a time for feasts. Chinese families share sweet, smooth rice cakes. Some families eat a whole cooked fish. They give oranges as presents. They eat noodles, too. These foods are symbols for a happy year and long life.

4   In most big cities families watch the Lunar New Year parade. Dragon dancers glide down the street. Lion dancers wear costumes in red, yellow, and green. Bands march by in rows. Their drums beat out happy tunes. People in traditional costumes go by on floats. They wave to the crowd. BANG! Watch out for firecrackers! They are part of the tradition, too. Loud sounds are symbols of a joyful time of year.

Literature Anthology:
pages 46–49

Reread and use the prompts to take notes in the text.

Reread paragraph 1. Draw a star before the sentence that explains what the Lunar New Year means. Write it here.

_____

_____

Now reread paragraphs 2–4. **Underline** Lunar New Year traditions.

COLLABORATE

Talk with a partner about Chinese New Year traditions. **Circle** words the author uses to help you picture things you might see at a Lunar New Year feast and parade.

Storytelling and Dance

1   Many Native American cultures have traditions of storytelling and dance. The stories are from long ago. Older people tell the stories to their children and grandchildren. They may use the culture's native language. The stories explain things in nature. They tell about the courage of early people.

2   Some Native American groups get together in the summer. They meet at big powwows. These festivals celebrate culture through dance and music. Storytellers bring the old tales to life. The soft notes of a flute may help tell a story. The firm beat of a drum adds power. People from other cultures can watch and listen. Everyone enjoys the stories and learns about the traditions.

Reread paragraph 1. **Circle** two Native American traditions. Which tradition does the paragraph describe?

_____

Underline two things the Native American stories are about.

With a partner, reread paragraph 2. Talk about how the author describes powwows. **Draw a box around** the things you might hear at a powwow.

How does the author help you picture what different traditions are like?

 Talk About It Look back at your notes. Talk with a partner about what you've learned about different traditions.

Cite Text Evidence What words does the author use to help you picture ways families share traditions? Write them in the web.

Quick Tip

Look back at the words you underlined in "Celebrating a New Year" and circled in "Storytelling and Dance." Think about which of these words best describe each tradition.

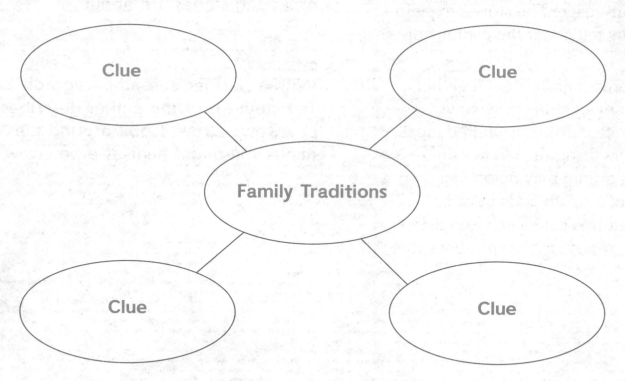

Clue

Clue

Family Traditions

Clue

Clue

Write The author helps me picture what traditions are like by

_____

_____

Voice

A writer chooses words and phrases that express what he or she thinks and feels about a topic. This use of language gives each writer his or her own voice.

 FIND TEXT EVIDENCE

*On page 47 of the **Literature Anthology**, the author of "Family Traditions" uses words and phrases like "drums beat out happy tunes" and "BANG!" This helps me see that the author finds the celebration fun and exciting.*

> Bands march by in rows. Their drums beat out happy tunes. People in traditional costumes go by on floats. They wave to the crowd. BANG! Watch out for firecrackers!

 Your Turn Reread the last paragraph on page 49.

- What phrases does the author use to describe traditions?

  _____

- How do these phrases contribute to the author's voice?

  _____

  _____

Readers to Writers

Choose your words and phrases carefully when you write. Your words and how you arrange them will let readers know how you feel about a topic.

Text Connections

? **How is the family in the photograph like the families in *Yoon and the Jade Bracelet* and "Family Traditions"?**

Talk About It With a partner, talk about what the family in the photograph is doing. Choose one clue that shows a tradition and talk about how you know it's important.

Cite Text Evidence Look at the photograph. Think about what is special to Yoon's mother and how the families in "Family Traditions" celebrate special days. **Circle** clues that show that the dinner is special. Then read the caption. **Draw a box around** text that helps you know this is a family tradition.

Write The families in the photograph and

selections are similar because _____

_____

_____

_____

_____

Find clues that show how the people in the photograph feel. This will help you compare how families celebrate traditions.

This family lives in Richmond, Virginia. They celebrate every Thanksgiving at their grandmother's house.

Digital Vision/Alamy

Present Your Work

Decide how you will present your culture quilt square to the class. Find out if it can be projected onto a large screen. Use the checklist to improve your presentation.

The most interesting thing I learned about my family's

tradition is _____

_____

_____

I would like to know more about _____

_____

_____

Quick Tip

Be sure to hold your drawing up so your audience can see it. As you talk about your family's tradition, point to related details in your illustration to help the audience better understand what your family does and why.

Presenting Checklist

☐ I will practice my presentation.

☐ I will make eye contact with the audience.

☐ I will speak loudly enough for everyone to hear me.

☐ I will hold up my drawing and point out key details in it.

Martin Luther King Jr. played an important role in American history. This monument in Washington, DC, honors his life. People visit monuments like this one to learn about important people and events in history. Landmarks and monuments help us remember and understand history.

Look at the photograph. Ask your partner questions about how monuments help people learn about history. Listen carefully, then write your ideas in the word web.

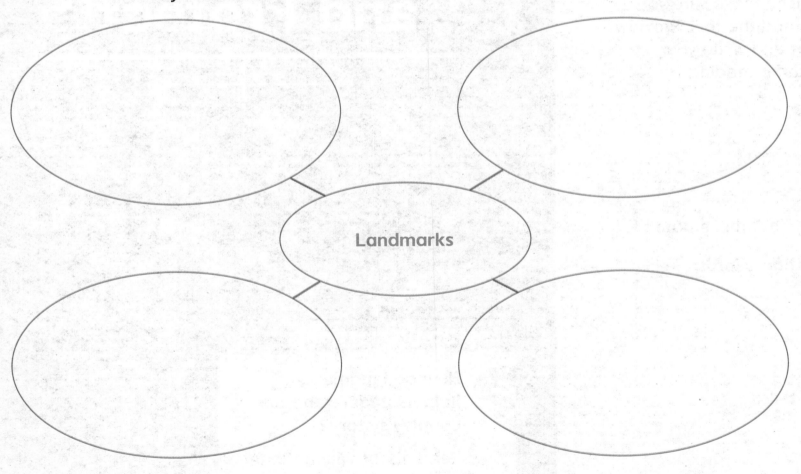

Landmarks

Go online to **my.mheducation.com** and read the "Special Places" Blast. Think about what makes a landmark stand out. Then blast back your response.

TAKE NOTES

Understanding why you are reading helps you adjust how you read. If you are reading for information, you might reread sections to make sure you understand the text. Preview the text and write your purpose for reading.

_____

_____

_____

As you read, make note of

Interesting Words: _____

_____

_____

Key Details: _____

_____

_____

_____

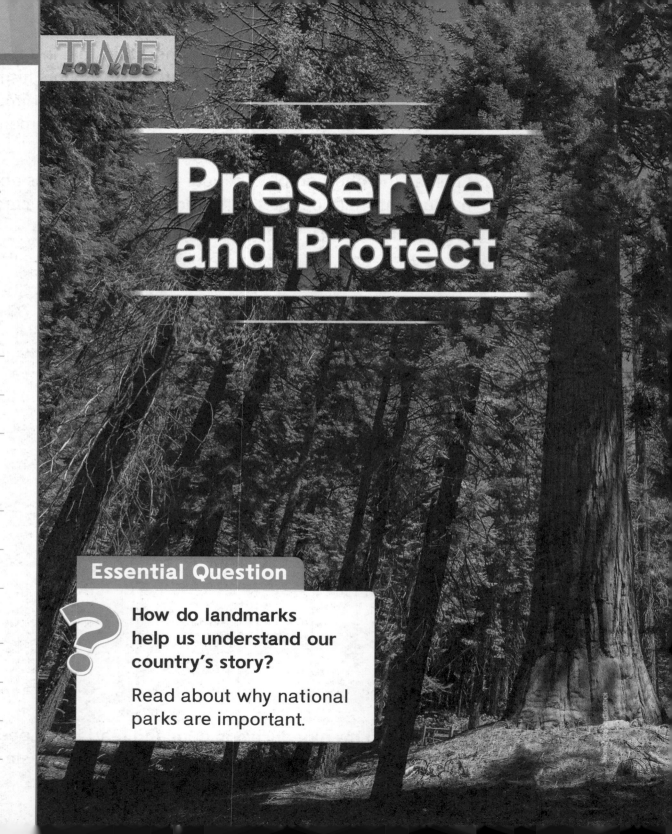

TIME FOR KIDS.

Preserve and Protect

Essential Question

How do landmarks help us understand our country's story?

Read about why national parks are important.

The largest living tree in the world lives in a forest in California. But not just any forest. This **massive** tree lives in the Giant Forest. It is a **landmark** that has been growing there for over 2,000 years. Many people work hard to protect this **national** treasure. There are rules to make sure this happens. But some people worry that there are too many rules.

A GIANT FOREST

More than one million people hike the trails in the Giant Forest to visit the General Sherman Tree each year. It's no wonder. The **grand** sequoia tree stands 275 feet tall. It is almost as wide as a school bus is long. But many other huge trees live there, too. The Giant Forest is where half of the Earth's sequoia trees live.

In 1964, President Lyndon B. Johnson signed a law that protects trees like the General Sherman. It also protects all plants and animals living in national parks. The law states that animals and wildlife are safe there. No one can cut trees or build homes on the land. The **traces**, or parts, of cultures that lived there long ago are protected. National parks protect thousands and thousands of acres of wildlife. But some people believe these lands should be available for other uses.

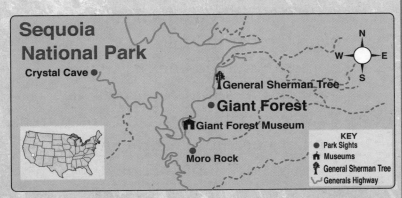

Sequoia National Park
Crystal Cave
General Sherman Tree
Giant Forest
Giant Forest Museum
Moro Rock

N W E S

KEY
● Park Sights
🏛 Museums
🌲 General Sherman Tree
〰 Generals Highway

The Sequoia National Park is located in California.

ARGUMENTATIVE TEXT

FIND TEXT EVIDENCE

Read

Paragraph 1
Ask and Answer Questions
What are some people worried about? **Underline** text evidence. Now think of a question you might have. Write it here.

_____

_____

Paragraph 2
Main Idea and Key Details
Circle three key details that tell about the Giant Forest.

Map

Look at the map key. **Draw a box around** the General Sherman tree. Write the name of another place on the map.

_____

Reread

Author's Craft

Why is "A Giant Forest" a good title for this section?

SHARED READ

FIND TEXT EVIDENCE

Read

Paragraph 1

Main Idea and Key Details

Underline three details that tell what the rules protect.

Paragraph 2

Multiple-Meaning Words

Draw a box around clues that help you figure out what *past* means. Write what it means.

Paragraph 3

Ask and Answer Questions

Ask a question about the lumber business. Write it here.

Reread

Author's Craft

How does the author help you understand how people who want to protect the land feel?

TIME FOR KIDS

POINT COUNTERPOINT

Protect the Land!

Millions of people visit national parks each year. Nature lovers hike the trails. They explore caves **carved** out of mountains. They admire hundreds of different plants and animals. These people agree with President Johnson. They like the rules that protect the land. They believe the rules help keep our country's forests and animals safe. They think all people should visit and enjoy them. They think people can learn from nature.

Visiting a national **monument** is a way to learn about history. Monuments preserve traces of past cultures so that they don't get destroyed. Scientists rely on these **clues** to help them learn about how people lived long ago.

COUNTERPOINT POINT

What About My Business?

Other people think there are too many rules that protect the land. They believe those rules hurt business owners. People need lumber to build new homes. Some businesses make lumber, or wood, from trees. If

Lumber businesses rely on trees to make money.

these companies can't cut down trees, the price of lumber goes up. That means things built with wood cost more to buy. Some people think the rules also make it harder for people to find jobs. People who cut down trees or build new houses have to find new jobs.

abadonian/iStock/Getty Images

To Protect or Not to Protect?

Today the United States has hundreds of national parks, monuments, and landmarks. Animals and plants live in them. Visitors enjoy them. Scientists learn from them. The rules protect them. But are there too many rules? Not everyone agrees.

Is It a Park or a Monument?

A United States national monument is a protected area. It is like a national park, but easier to create. Monuments and parks are different in other important ways.

National Parks

- are large natural places with many different natural features
- aim to protect many different aspects of nature

National Monuments

- often focus on protecting one specific natural resource, landmark, or structure that has historic or scientific interest
- receive less money and less wildlife protection than parks

Summarize

Use your notes and think about the facts in "Preserve and Protect." Summarize the main ideas of each claim.

ARGUMENTATIVE TEXT

FIND TEXT EVIDENCE

Read

Paragraph 1

Multiple-Meaning Words

Find the word *parks*. **Circle** clues that help you figure out its meaning. Write what it means.

Sidebar

Main Ideas and Key Details

Underline details that tell what a national monument is.

Sidebars

What information does the sidebar give you? **Draw a box around** text evidence.

Reread

Author's Craft

How does the sidebar help you understand how monuments and parks are different?

Vocabulary

Use the sentences to talk with a partner about each word. Then answer the questions.

carved

An artist **carved** the statue out of rock.

What other things can be carved?

_____

_____

clues

Paw prints are **clues** that an animal walked by recently.

What clues tell you that it might rain?

_____

_____

Build Your Word List Pick one of the interesting words you listed on page 62. Use a print or online dictionary to find the word's meaning. Then use the word in a sentence.

grand

The family sat and gazed at the **grand** view of the river.

What else would make a grand view?

_____

_____

landmark

The Statue of Liberty is an American **landmark**.

What other landmarks can you name?

_____

_____

massive

The boaters looked up at the **massive** cliff.

What is another word for massive?

_____

_____

monument

Mount Rushmore is a **monument** that honors the leaders of our country.

Describe a monument you have seen.

_____

_____

national

The Fourth of July is a **national** holiday.

Name another national holiday.

_____

_____

traces

In the morning we found **traces**, or small amounts, of snow on the plants.

What does traces mean?

_____

_____

Multiple-Meaning Words

Multiple-meaning words have more than one meaning. Find other words in the sentence, or beyond the sentence, to help you figure out the meaning of a multiple-meaning word.

FIND TEXT EVIDENCE

On page 63 I see the word feet. _This word can mean "the things humans walk on" or "a measure of length." The context clues "stands" and "tall" help me figure out that_ feet _refers to the length of something._

The grand sequoia tree **stands** 275 feet **tall.**

Your Turn Use context clues to figure out the meanings of the following words.

plants, _page 64_ _____

safe, _page 64_ _____

Ask and Answer Questions

Stop and ask yourself questions as you read. Then look for details to support your answers. This will help you gain information.

FIND TEXT EVIDENCE

Reread the section "Protect the Land!" on page 64. Think of a question. Then reread to answer it.

Page 64

TIME FOR KIDS.

Protect the Land!

Millions of people visit national parks each year. Nature lovers hike the trails. They explore caves **carved** out of mountains. They admire hundreds of different plants and animals. These people agree with President Johnson. They like the rules that protect the land. They believe the rules help keep our country's forests and animals safe. They think all people should visit and enjoy them. They think people can learn from nature.

Visiting a national **monument** is a way to learn about history. Monuments preserve traces of past cultures so that they don't get destroyed. Scientists rely on these **clues** to help them learn about how people lived long ago.

What About My Business?

Other people think there are

I have a question. What do people do when they visit national parks? I read that people hike the trails. They explore caves. They admire the plants and animals. Now I can answer my question. People visit national parks for many reasons.

Your Turn Reread the first paragraph on page 65. Think of one question. You might ask, *How do the rules hurt business owners?* Write your question below. Read the section again to find the answer and write it.

_____

_____

Captions, Maps, and Sidebars

"Preserve and Protect" is an **argumentative text**.

Argumentative text

- is nonfiction stating the author's opinion on a topic
- gives facts and examples to persuade the reader to agree with the author's opinion, or claim
- may include text features such as captions, maps, and sidebars

FIND TEXT EVIDENCE

I can tell that "Preserve and Protect" is an argumentative text. It has points for and counterpoints against protecting wild land. It includes facts about why the land should be protected and why it should be used as a resource by businesses.

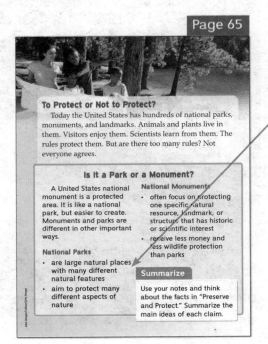

Page 65

To Protect or Not to Protect?

Today the United States has hundreds of national parks, monuments, and landmarks. Animals and plants live in them. Visitors enjoy them. Scientists learn from them. The rules protect them. But are there too many rules? Not everyone agrees.

Is It a Park or a Monument?

A United States national monument is a protected area. It is like a national park, but easier to create. Monuments and parks are different in other important ways.

National Parks
- are large natural places with many different natural features
- aim to protect many different aspects of nature

National Monuments
- often focus on protecting one specific natural resource, landmark, or structure that has historic or scientific interest
- receive less money and less wildlife protection than parks

Summarize

Use your notes and think about the facts in "Preserve and Protect." Summarize the main ideas of each claim.

Captions

Captions give extra information that is not in a text.

Sidebar

A sidebar gives more information about a topic.

COLLABORATE

Your Turn Find more text features in "Preserve and Protect." What else did you learn? Write your answer below.

_____

_____

Main Idea and Key Details

The main, or central, idea is the most important point the author makes about a topic. Key details tell about the main idea.

🔍 FIND TEXT EVIDENCE

What details tell about why many people support protecting the land? I can reread "Protect the Land!" on page 64 and find important details. Then I can figure out what these details have in common to tell the main idea.

Quick Tip

The heading of the section often gives a clue about what the main idea is. Think about what the key details have in common and how they relate to the heading. Then use them to tell the main idea of this section of the text.

Main Idea
Millions of people agree that rules protect the land.
Detail
They believe rules keep our forests and animals safe.
Detail
They think all people should visit and enjoy them.

Your Turn Reread "What About My Business?" on page 64. Find details about why many business owners think there are too many rules. List these details in your graphic organizer.

Juice Images/Cultura/Getty Images.

Main Idea
Detail
Detail
Detail

Respond to Reading

Talk about the prompt below. Think about how the author helps you see both sides of the argument. Use your notes and graphic organizer.

How does the author help you understand both claims of the argument about protecting land?

_____

_____

_____

_____

_____

_____

_____

_____

_____

_____

Quick Tip

Use these sentence starters to talk about protecting land.

I read that some people think . . .

I read that business owners think . . .

The author uses text features to . . .

Grammar Connections

As you write your response be sure to use a variety of sentences, including simple and compound sentences. Remember to use the correct punctuation and conjunction in each compound sentence.

Facts and Opinions

When you try to convince the reader to think a certain way or do something, it is important to list reasons that support your opinion, or claim. The most effective reasons are usually facts. **Facts** are statements that can be proven true. **Opinions** are statements based on feelings.

Quick Tip

People send postcards to their family and friends. Include facts and opinions that would make your friends want to visit this place.

1 Look at the postcard. Write two facts here:

_____

_____

2 How do you know they are facts? Write your ideas here:

_____

_____

Now reread the postcard. Write an opinion here:

_____

The General Sherman tree is very old. It is 275 feet tall. This tree is amazing and you should go see it!

Create a Postcard Research a Texas landmark or monument and create a postcard explaining why people should visit it.

1. On one side of the postcard, draw a picture of the landmark.
2. On the other side, write a paragraph telling why people should visit it. Be sure to include two or three facts about the landmark or monument and your opinion.

Protecting Our Parks

Literature Anthology:
pages 50–53

? **How does the author help you understand why the National Park System is important?**

Talk About It Reread **Literature Anthology** page 51. Talk with a partner about what the National Park System does.

Cite Text Evidence What facts does the author use to show that the National Park System is important? Write them here.

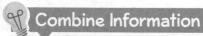

Combine Information

Use what you know about protecting wildlife and the facts the author gives to help you understand why the National Park System is important.

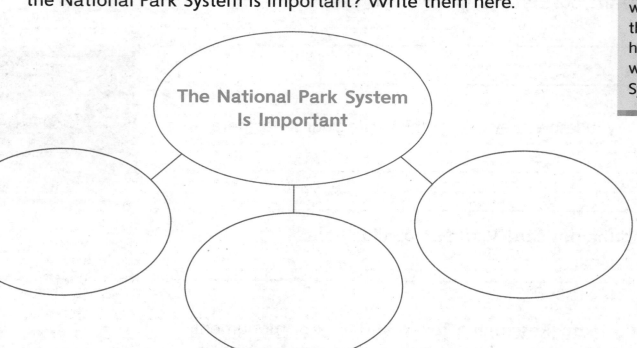

The National Park System Is Important

Write I understand why the National Park System is important

because the author _____

_____

? **How does the author help you understand the different opinions, or claims, people have about park visitors?**

Talk About It Reread pages 52–53. Talk with a partner about the opinions expressed in "Allow All Access" and "Protect Our Parks."

Cite Text Evidence What facts support each opinion or claim? Write them in the chart.

Allow All Access	Protect Our Parks

Write I understand the different claims people have about park visitors because the author _____

_____

_____

_____

_____

Quick Tip

When you read an argumentative text, think about who the intended audience or reader might be. Ask yourself, "Who is the author trying to convince or persuade?"

Make Inference

By using evidence from the text and your own experience with other argumentative texts, make an inference about who the intended audience, or reader, is for "Protecting Our Parks."

Respond to Reading

Answer the prompt below. Think about how overcrowding affects national parks. Use your notes and graphic organizer.

How does the author help you understand how national parks need to change to deal with overcrowding?

_____

_____

_____

_____

_____

_____

_____

_____

_____

_____

Quick Tip

Use these sentence starters to talk about national parks.

I read that overcrowding . . .

Some people think . . .

Other people think . . .

Self-Selected Reading

Choose a text. In your writer's notebook, write the title, author, and genre of the book. As you read, make a connection to ideas in other texts you have read or to a personal experience. Write your ideas in your notebook.

5 Questions for George McDonald

Literature Anthology:
pages 54–55

The National Park Service recently celebrated its 100th anniversary. George McDonald is the park service's youth programs manager. He spoke with TFK's Elizabeth Winchester.

The Find Your Park program encourages families to visit parks and share their experiences. Why?

It is important for young people and their families to identify with these magnificent places because they belong to everyone. Find Your Park encourages more people to appreciate our country's valuable resources, and to also protect them.

The Every Kid in a Park program gives free admission to the families of fourth graders. Why?

Reaching kids at this age increases their chances for academic success.

Reread and use the prompts to take notes in the text.

Reread the first two questions and answers. **Circle** the names of national park programs that are important to George McDonald. Write them here.

_____

_____

COLLABORATE

Reread the introduction with a partner. **Underline** details that tell you more about George McDonald and his connection to national parks. Talk about why the author chose him to answer questions about national parks.

? How do you know that George McDonald thinks it is important for young people to visit national parks?

Talk About It Reread the excerpt on page 77. Talk with a partner about the Find Your Park and Every Kid in a Park programs.

Cite Text Evidence What claims does George McDonald make with each program to convince young people to visit national parks? Write text evidence in the chart.

Reread the excerpt on page 77.

Find Your Park	Every Kid in a Park

Write I know that George McDonald thinks it's important for

young people to visit national parks because _____

_____

_____

_____

_____

> **Quick Tip**
>
> A claim is something a person says is true. Authors use facts or opinions to prove their claims. Facts are true. Opinions are what a person thinks about something.

Author's Purpose

An author's purpose is his or her reason for writing a text. It could be to inform by providing facts about a topic, entertain by telling a story, or persuade the reader to agree with an opinion.

 FIND TEXT EVIDENCE

On page 77, the author begins "5 Questions with George McDonald" by stating that George works for the National Park Service. This fact helps me understand that the author's purpose is to inform readers about George and the work that he does.

George McDonald is the park service's youth programs manager.

 Your Turn Reread page 55 in the **Literature Anthology**. How does the author help you know more about the landmarks?

_____

_____

What is the author's purpose for writing about the landmarks? How do you know?

_____

_____

Readers to Writers

Think about your purpose for writing. If you are writing to inform your readers, include facts that help them learn more about your topic.

Text Connections

? **How is the message of the illustration below like the message of "Protecting Our Parks" and "5 Questions for George McDonald"?**

Talk About It With a partner, talk about what you see in the illustration. Choose some of the things you see and discuss why people would want to visit this place.

Cite Text Evidence **Circle** two things in the illustration you talked about with your partner. Read the caption. **Underline** clues in the caption that inform people about America.

Write The messages of F. F. Palmer's painting and the texts I read this week are alike

because _____

_____

_____

_____

_____

_____

F. F. Palmer is known for her illustrations of American life. She created "The Mountain Pass" in 1867. It shows the Sierra Nevada mountain range, one of America's most beautiful landmarks and the center of the California gold rush, which began in 1848.

Accuracy and Phrasing

When reading an argumentative text aloud, read facts, such as dates and numbers, with accuracy so the audience hears them correctly. Read as though you are speaking naturally. Pause at commas and periods. Use expression when you see question marks and exclamation points. This kind of phrasing helps your audience pay attention.

Quick Tip

Don't rush when you read facts aloud. Read at a rate that helps your listeners understand the facts and how they relate to the topic.

Page 51

No one knew that millions of people would want to visit. There were no clues. Now more than 275 million visitors come to the parks and monuments each year!

Read numbers with accuracy.

Use appropriate expression when you see an exclamation point.

Your Turn Turn to page 51 in the **Literature Anthology**. Take turns reading the first and second paragraphs of "Too Many Visitors" aloud with a partner. Pay attention to the facts, numbers, and punctuation. Read accurately.

Afterward think about how you did. Complete these sentences.

I remembered to _____

_____

Next time I will _____

_____

WRITING

Expert Model

Literature Anthology:
pages 50–53

Features of Persuasive Essay

A **persuasive essay** is a kind of argumentative text. A persuasive essay

- clearly states the writer's opinion, or claim, in the opening
- supports the writer's claim with facts and examples
- tries to convince readers to agree with the writer's claim

Analyze an Expert Model Reread page 51 of "Protecting Our Parks" in the **Literature Anthology**. Use text evidence to answer these questions.

How do you know the author thinks it is important to protect national

parks? _____

_____

How does the author try to convince readers that national parks

need more protection? _____

_____

_____

_____

Word Wise

"Protecting Our Parks" gives points for, and counterpoints against, the argument that national parks should be open to all visitors. A persuasive essay usually picks one claim and gives facts and opinions to support the argument.

Plan: Choose Your Topic

COLLABORATE

Brainstorm With a partner, think of some national parks or landmarks. Why might visiting these places help you learn about our country? Use these sentence starters to talk about your ideas.

A U.S. park or landmark I know is . . .

One reason to visit this place is . . .

Writing Prompt Choose one of the parks or landmarks you discussed as your topic for a persuasive essay. You will need to convince your readers that this is an important place to visit to learn about America.

I will write about _____

Purpose and Audience An author's purpose is the main reason for writing. Your audience is who will be reading what you write.

The reason I am writing about this topic is _____

_____

_____

_____

Quick Tip

When you write a persuasive essay, you are trying to convince your audience to agree with your claim. As you plan your essay, ask yourself: *What facts will persuade my readers to visit the place that I am writing about? Where can I find these facts?*

Plan Think about what you want your readers to learn about the place you are writing about. Why should they visit? Ask yourself questions and answer them in your writer's notebook.

Plan: Research

Identify Relevant Information You will need to research your topic before you begin to write. Use encyclopedias, Web sites, books, and electronic sources to gather information about your park or landmark. Ask an adult to help you plan your research and figure out which sources to use. Make sure you find facts and examples that are relevant, or related to, your topic.

Work with an adult to write three steps in your research plan.

1. _____

2. _____

3. _____

List two sources you will use here.

_____

_____

 Take Notes In your writer's notebook, draw a Main Idea and Details chart. Take notes and write three details that support your claim in your chart.

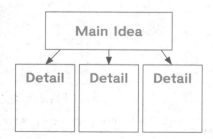

Draft

Fact and Opinion Writers use facts to support their claims. Facts are true and can be proved. Opinions are beliefs that might or might not be true. In the example below from "Protecting Our Parks," the author uses facts to support a claim.

> The National Park Service thinks that people should be able to visit America's parks and landmarks. Their mission is to protect land so that it can be enjoyed by everyone. They want families to hike the trails, observe the animals, and learn about our country's history. But visitors need bathrooms, parking lots, and places to eat.

Now use the above paragraph as a model to write about the park or landmark you chose for your topic. Remember to use facts.

_____

_____

_____

_____

_____

_____

Write a Draft Look over your Main Idea and Details chart. Use it to write your draft in your writer's notebook. Remember to clearly state your claim, then use facts to support it.

Quick Tip

When using facts to support your claim, be sure to paraphrase, or put them into your own words. Read the fact a few times to make sure you understand it. Then explain it using your own words.

Revise

Quick Tip

Think about the facts you learned while researching your topic. Which fact grabbed your attention? Use it to write a strong opening that makes your audience want to learn more.

Strong Opening Persuasive essays that have a strong opening begin by clearly stating the writer's opinion. They also grab the reader's attention so that he or she will want to keep reading.

Reread the first two paragraphs of "Protecting Our Parks" on page 51 of the **Literature Anthology**. Talk with a partner about how the author grabs your attention. Write about it here.

_____

_____

_____

Revise It's time to revise your writing. Read your draft and think about ways you might

- state your opinion more clearly

- include facts that grab the reader's attention

Circle two sentences in your draft that you can change. Revise and write them here.

1 _____

_____

2 _____

Peer Conferences

COLLABORATE

Review a Draft Listen carefully as a partner reads his or her draft aloud. Tell what you like about the draft. Use these sentence starters to help you discuss your partner's draft.

I like the way you started your essay because . . .

Add another fact here to . . .

You did/did not convince me because . . .

I have a question about . . .

Partner Feedback After you take turns giving each other feedback, write one of your partner's suggestions that you will use in your revision.

_____

_____

_____

_____

Revision After you finish your peer conference, use the Revising Checklist to figure out what you can change to make your persuasive essay better. Remember to use the rubric on page 89 to help with your revision.

Tech Tip

The program you use to write your draft on a computer should include a thesaurus. The thesaurus will help you find synonyms for words you might want to replace. Using new words instead of repeating old ones can make your essay more interesting to read.

Edit and Proofread

After you revise your persuasive essay, proofread it to find any mistakes in grammar, spelling, and punctuation. Read your draft at least three times. This will help you catch any mistakes. Use the checklist below to edit your sentences.

✔ Editing Checklist

- [ ] Do all sentences start with a capital letter and end with a punctuation mark?
- [ ] Are the names of specific parks or landmarks capitalized?
- [ ] Are both simple and compound sentences used?
- [ ] Are all words spelled correctly?

List two mistakes that you found as you proofread your persuasive essay.

1 _____

_____

_____

2 _____

_____

_____

Grammar Connections

When you proofread your draft for mistakes, remember that using a combination of both simple and compound sentences will make your essay more interesting. A simple sentence is a complete sentence made of a subject and a verb. A compound sentence is made of two simple sentences joined by words such as *and*, *but*, *or*, and *so*.

Publish, Present, and Evaluate

Publishing When you publish your writing, you create a neat final copy that is free of mistakes. If you are not using a computer, use your best handwriting. Write legibly in print or cursive.

Presentation When you are ready to present, practice your presentation. Use the Presenting Checklist.

Evaluate After you publish, use the rubric to evaluate your writing.

What did you do well? _____

_____

What could use some improvement? _____

_____

4	3	2	1
• claim is clearly stated in a strong opening • includes several supporting facts • very few spelling, grammar, or punctuation errors	• claim is clearly stated • includes supporting facts • some spelling, grammar, or punctuation errors	• claim is somewhat unclear • includes few supporting facts • several spelling, grammar, and punctuation errors	• claim is not stated • includes only one supporting fact • many spelling, grammar and punctuation errors

SHOW WHAT YOU LEARNED

Spiral Review

You have learned new skills and strategies in Unit 1 that will help you read more critically. Now it is time to practice what you have learned.

- **Headings**
- **Maps**
- **Main Idea and Key Details**
- **Compound Words**
- **Character, Setting, Plot: Sequence**
- **Dialogue**
- **Visualize**
- **Context Clues**

Connect to Content

- **Create a Venn Diagram**
- **Write an Advertisement**
- **Reading Digitally**

Read the selection and choose the best answer to each question.

☆ Remembering ☆

San Jacinto

1   The world's tallest column monument reaches high in LaPorte, Texas. This landmark is over 565 feet tall. It honors the victory that took place there in 1836. The win led to the independence of Texas from Mexico.

The Battle of San Jacinto

2   In the 1820s, Mexico gained its independence from Spain. Soon, Mexicans welcomed Americans to settle in Texas. In time, however, Americans outnumbered Mexicans. The Mexicans worried they might lose Texas. They decided to close Texas to new settlers.

3   Over the next few years, Texans grew tired of the Mexican government. They wanted to be free. In October 1835, they started the Texas Revolution. It included battles at the Alamo and at Goliad. The Texans lost both.

4   The Texans decided to launch a surprise attack on Mexican troops. The Mexicans had about 1,500 troops. The Texans had just 800. On April 21, 1836, the Texans sneaked up on the Mexican troops. They hid behind trees and the hilly landscape. Then they attacked.

5   After just 18 minutes, the Texans had victory in sight. Within 24 hours, they had captured about 700 Mexicans, including their general. He was set free after he agreed to end the war. Only six Texans died.

Visiting the Monument

6   Construction of the monument began on the 100th anniversary of the battle. It opened exactly three years later. The landmark honors all who fought for the independence of Texas.

7   Today you can visit the San Jacinto battlefield and the monument that towers over it. The column has a large star at the top and a museum at its base. You can ride an elevator 489 feet up. Then you can look out over the battlefield, Houston, and San Jacinto Bay.

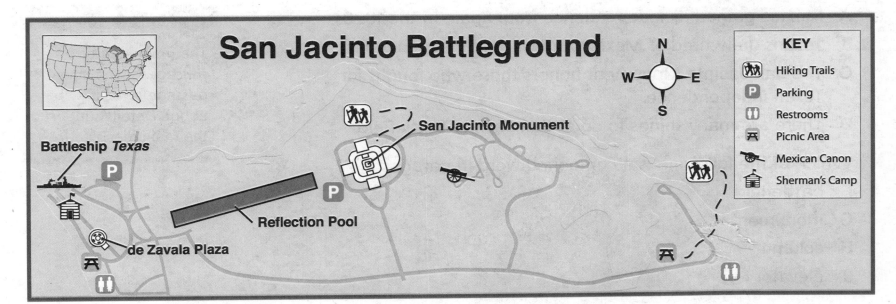

San Jacinto Battleground

KEY
- 🚶 Hiking Trails
- 🅿 Parking
- 🚻 Restrooms
- 🪑 Picnic Area
- Mexican Canon
- 🏠 Sherman's Camp

Battleship *Texas*

San Jacinto Monument

Reflection Pool

de Zavala Plaza

© David R. Frazier Photolibrary, Inc. / Alamy

SHOW WHAT YOU LEARNED

1 What information would you expect to find under the heading "The Battle of San Jacinto"?

   A a description of the monument

   B the date the battle took place

   C things to do today at the site

   D the height of the elevator to the top

2 Look at the map. Use the compass rose. Start at the San Jacinto Monument. Which direction is the Battleship *Texas*?

   F east

   G west

   H north

   J south

3 What is the main idea of the passage?

   A Mexico gained its independence from Spain in the 1820s.

   B Texans grew tired of Mexico and wanted independence.

   C The San Jacinto Monument honors those who fought for Texan independence.

   D There are many things to do at San Jacinto Battlefield.

4 Which of the following is a compound word in paragraph 7?

   F battlefield

   G monument

   H column

   J elevator

> **Quick Tip**
>
> The main idea of a passage is what the passage is mostly about. Details support the main idea.

Read the selection and choose the best answer to each question.

Sofia's Mexican Birthday

1   Mama cracked open Sofia's bedroom door. "Guess who's here for your birthday."

2   Sofia's brown eyes grew wide. "Who?" she asked.

3   "Abuela!" Mama said as she pushed the door open wide.

4   Sofia bounced off her bed like a spring. It had been more than a year since she'd seen her grandmother.

5   "Abuela, you came from Mexico to celebrate with me?"

6   "You bet!" Abuela said. "Now tell me about your party."

7   "I'm not sure what to do," Sofia said.

8   "In Mexico, birthdays are always a big celebration!" Abuela said. "We invited everyone to your mama's party."

9   "I want to have a Mexican birthday party!" Sofia squealed. "What else did Mama do for her birthday?"

10   "I made tortilla chips and salsa and taquitos to eat."

11   "What are taquitos?" Sofia wanted to know.

12   "They're rolled tortillas filled with meat," said Abuela.

13   "Did Mama have a birthday cake?" Sofia asked.

14   "She wanted flan instead," Abuela said.

15 "What's that?" Sofia asked.

16 "Flan is like custard with a sweet caramel sauce on top," explained Abuela. "It's so creamy and smooth on the tongue!"

17 "Can you make flan for my party?" asked Sofia.

18 "Of course!" said Abuela.

19 "Did Mama play games?" Sofia asked.

20 "It's not a birthday party in Mexico without a piñata," said Abuela. "We hung the candy-filled container from a tree. Then we blindfolded one guest at a time, and he or she swung at the piñata with a stick until someone broke it open—*crack!* Candy rained down, and everyone dove to the ground to get some!"

21 "I want a piñata, too!" said Sofia.

22 Over the next week, Sofia and Abuela got ready for the party. Abuela showed Sofia how to make her own tortilla chips, salsa, and taquitos. Sofia helped her make flan, too. They even made their own piñata in the shape of a donkey.

23 "I'm so happy you came to America for my party, Abuela," Sofia said. "I want to have a Mexican birthday party every year!"

1 Who is speaking in paragraph 1?

A a narrator

B Abuela

C Sofia

D Mama

2 What does Abuela describe first about Mexican birthdays?

F guests

G flan

H taquitos

J piñatas

3 What context clue in paragraph 16 tells you what flan is?

A creamy

B custard

C delicious

D caramel

4 Which word in paragraph 20 helps readers use their sense of hearing to visualize what is happening?

F rained

G blindfolded

H crack

J piñata

> **Quick Tip**
>
> Context clues are words and phrases that help readers figure out the meaning of unfamiliar words. Look for context clues in surrounding sentences.

COMPARING GENRES

COLLABORATE

- In the **Literature Anthology**, reread the narrative nonfiction text *Gary the Dreamer* on pages 10–21, and the argumentative text "Protecting Our Parks" on pages 50–53.

- Use the Venn diagram below to show how the two genres are the same and different.

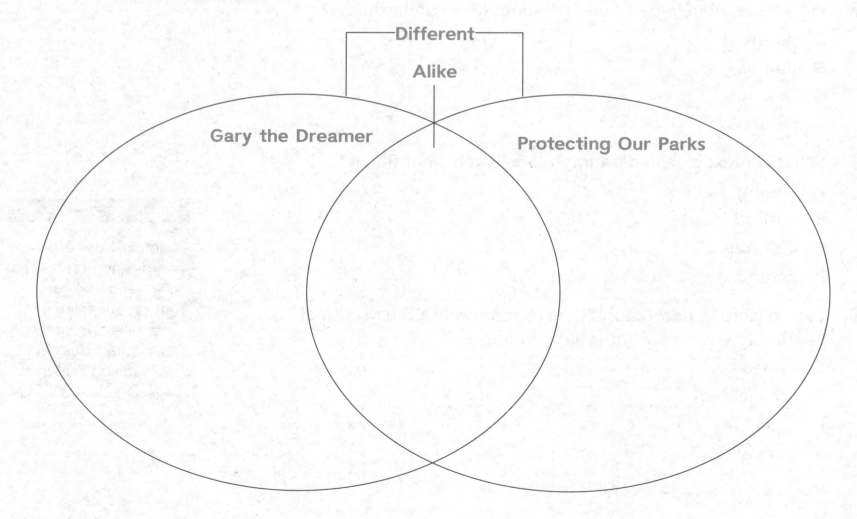

Different

Alike

Gary the Dreamer

Protecting Our Parks

HOMOGRAPHS

Homographs are words that are spelled the same but have different meanings. They are sometimes pronounced differently. You can use nearby words as clues to help you figure out the meaning of a homograph in a sentence.

- Read the sentences below and find the homograph.
- Use nearby words as clues to help you figure out the meaning of the homograph.

1 Last week I had a bad case of the flu and stayed home.

2 The museum kept the ancient coins in a glass case.

The homograph is _____

Circle the homograph in each sentence.

I used _____ to figure out the meaning of the

homograph in sentence I. The homograph means _____ .

_____

I used _____ to figure out the meaning of the

homograph in sentence 2. The homograph means _____ .

_____

EXTEND YOUR LEARNING

WRITE AN ADVERTISEMENT

The purpose of an advertisement is to persuade people to do something or buy a product. Write an ad persuading people to visit your favorite landmark. Tell your readers positive things about the landmark you want them to visit.

- Choose your favorite landmark to write about.
- Research facts about the landmark and write the ad.
- Draw a map of the landmark.

The landmark I decided to create an ad for is _____

I chose this landmark because _____

WRITE DIRECTIONS

When you write directions, you give step-by-step instructions for doing or making something. Directions often include time-order words like *first, next,* and *last*.

- Think of one thing you can share about a cultural celebration your family has.
- Write step-by-step directions about how to celebrate it.
- Read your instructions to a partner. Have your partner restate your directions. Then have your partner read his or her instructions to you. Restate them. Write one thing you learned about your partner's celebration.

_____

_____

READING DIGITALLY

Log on to **my.mheducation.com** and read the Time for Kids online article "Soccer Is America's Game" including the information found in the interactive elements. Answer the questions below.

Time for Kids: "Soccer Is America's Game"

• What is one claim, or opinion, in this text?

_____

_____

_____

• How does the author support this claim?

_____

_____

_____

• What readers do you think the author wrote this article for? Use text evidence to explain why.

_____

_____

_____

_____

strickke/E+/Getty Images

TRACK YOUR PROGRESS

WHAT DID YOU LEARN?

Use the rubric to evaluate yourself on the skills that you learned in this unit. Write your scores in the boxes below.

4	3	2	1
I can successfully identify all examples of this skill.	I can identify most examples of this skill.	I can identify a few examples of this skill.	I need to work on this skill more.

☐ Text Structure   ☐ Sequence   ☐ Main Idea and Details

☐ Compound Words   ☐ Context Clues   ☐ Multiple-Meaning Words

Something I need to work more on is _____ because

_____

_____

_____

Text-to-Self Think back over the texts that you have read in this unit. Choose one text and write a short paragraph explaining a personal connection that you have made to the text.

I made a personal connection to _____ because _____

_____

_____

Present Your Work

Use the Presenting Checklist to practice your presentation.
Discuss the sentence starters below and write your answers.

SPACE CENTER
HOUSTON

SUSAN LANE
35 FIRST STREET
ATLANTA, GEORGIA
35592

An interesting fact I learned about the landmark on my postcard is

_____

_____

I would like to know more about _____

_____

_____

Read your postcard to the class. After each of your classmates
presents, locate the landmark or monument on a map of Texas.
Highlight Austin, the state capital of Texas.

Quick Tip

Find or draw a larger version of the picture you put on your postcard. Display the larger version as you present your postcard so that your classmates can see the picture better.

✓ Presenting Checklist

☐ I will practice presenting my postcard.

☐ I will clearly name the landmark I am describing.

☐ I will explain the facts about the landmark.

☐ Then I will point out where the landmark is on a map.

BALLOT BOX

The students are voting for class president today. They vote for the person they think will do the best job. Voting lets people know what you think. It gives you the power to choose.

Look at the photograph. Talk about what the students are doing. Write what you see in the word web.

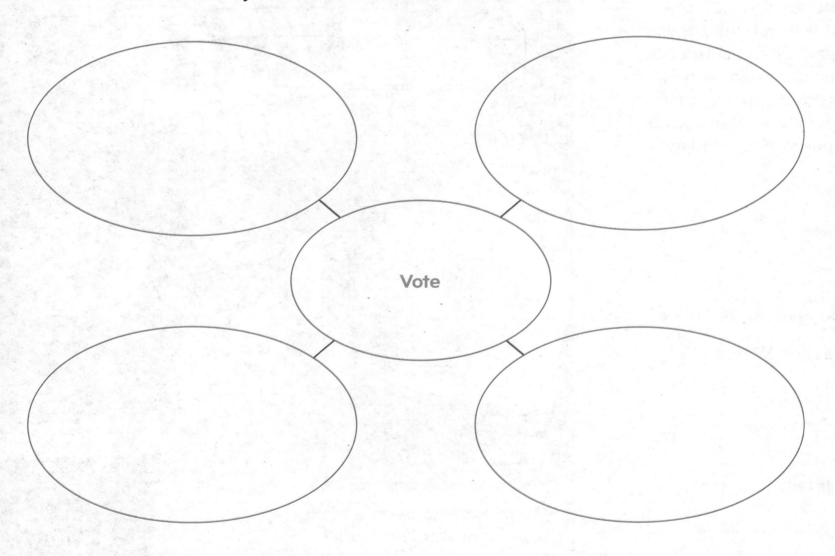

Vote

Go online to **my.mheducation.com** and read the "Let's Vote on It" Blast. Think about how voting can solve a problem. Then blast back your response.

TAKE NOTES

When you understand why you are reading, you can adjust how you read. If you are reading for information, you might reread sections to understand important facts. Preview the text and write your purpose for reading.

_____

_____

_____

As you read, make note of:

Interesting Words:_____

_____

_____

Key Details: _____

_____

_____

_____

Essential Question

? How do people make government work?

Read about a group that teaches kids the power of voting.

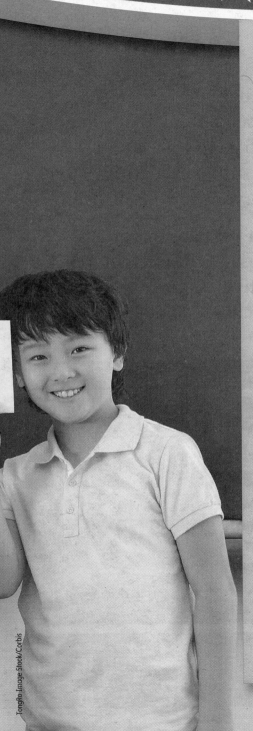

Have you ever voted? Maybe you voted to choose a class pet. Maybe your family voted on which movie to see. If you have ever voted, then you know how good it feels. Voting is important. It tells people what you think.

Many years ago, the leaders of our country wanted to know what people thought, too. They wrote a plan for our **government**. It is called the Constitution. It gives men and women in the United States the right to vote.

Each year, people who are eighteen years and older pick new leaders. They also vote on new laws. Voting gives Americans the power to choose.

FIND TEXT EVIDENCE

Read

Paragraph 1

Author's Point of View

What does the author think is important about voting? **Draw a box around** text evidence.

Paragraphs 2–3

Reread

What is the Constitution? **Circle** text evidence that tells what it is. **Underline** text that tells what it does. Write what it does here.

_____

_____

_____

_____

Reread

Author's Craft

How does the author help you understand the role voting plays in society?

TongRo Image Stock/Corbis

FIND TEXT EVIDENCE 🔍

Read

Paragraph 1

Author's Point of View

How does the author feel about people not voting?

_____

_____

Draw a box around text evidence.

Paragraph 2

Headings

What is the heading of this section? Write it here.

_____

_____

Underline text evidence that tells what Kids Voting USA does to teach kids to vote.

Teaching Kids to Vote

Fact

Did you know that only about six out of every ten Americans vote? That's sad. Some people think that voting is too hard. They are unsure where to go to vote. They think it takes too much time. Now, a group called Kids Voting USA is trying to **convince** everyone to vote.

Point of view

opinion

opinion

Kids Voting USA teaches kids that voting is important. The group gives teachers lessons to use in their classrooms. First, kids read stories and do fun activities about government. They also learn how to choose and **elect** a good leader.

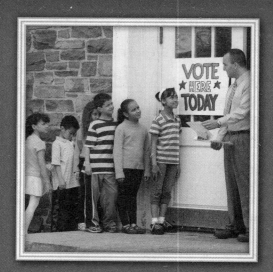

Election Day is here!

First we sign in.

Next, kids talk with their families. They reread stories about **candidates**. These are the people who want to be chosen as leaders. Families discuss their ideas and make **decisions**. That way, when it's time to vote, kids know whom they want to vote for.

On Election Day, kids get to vote just like adults. They use ballots like the ones in real elections. A ballot is a special form with the names of candidates on it. Kids mark their choices on the ballot. Then they put the ballot into a special box. Finally, all the votes are counted and recounted. The winners are **announced**, and everyone knows who won.

Then we mark a ballot.

Finally we vote!

FIND TEXT EVIDENCE

Read

Paragraph 1

Reread

Underline two things that help kids make decisions about whom to vote for.

Paragraph 2

Prefixes

Draw a box around *recounted*. Write the prefix here.

_____

What does *recounted* mean?

_____

Reread

Author's Craft

How does the author help you understand what a ballot is?

FIND TEXT EVIDENCE

Read

Paragraph 1

Reread

Underline how voting helps kids. Why does Kids Voting USA want kids to vote now?

_____

_____

Paragraph 2

Author's Point of View

What does the author think about voting?

_____

Circle text evidence to support your answer.

Reread

Author's Craft

How does the author use the caption to help you understand how kids are learning to vote?

Vote Now

Voting helps kids learn how to be **independent** and think for themselves. It also gives them the power to share how they feel. Kids Voting USA wants kids to vote now. There's a good reason. They **estimate** that when these kids grow up, more of them will vote.

In about ten years, kids your age will be old enough to vote. You will have the power to help elect great leaders and make new laws. Isn't that exciting?

Elections are held in many schools to teach kids how to vote.

This bar graph shows the results of a class election. Which pet was the favorite?

Vote for a Class Pet

Hamster
Hermit Crab
Guinea Pig
Mouse

0 1 2 3 4 5 6 7 8

Summarize

Use your notes and think about why voting is important. Summarize your ideas.

FIND TEXT EVIDENCE

Read

Paragraph 1

Reread

What does the bar graph show?

_____

_____

Underline text evidence.

Bar Graph

Look at the bar graph. **Circle** the pets in the class election. Which pet got the most votes?

_____

How many votes did it get?

_____

Reread

Author's Craft

How does the bar graph help you understand more about voting?

Vocabulary

Use the sentences to talk with a partner about each word. Then answer the questions.

announced

The teacher **announced** the winner of the election.

What is something that your teacher has announced?

_____

_____

candidates

Andrew was happy to be one of the **candidates** for class president.

What are some things candidates do before an election?

_____

_____

convince

Amir tried to **convince** his friend to play baseball.

What is something someone tried to convince you to do?

_____

_____

decisions

Jasmine made two **decisions** about what to eat for breakfast.

Name two decisions you make every day.

_____

_____

elect

The players voted to **elect** a team captain.

What is another word for elect?

_____

 Build Your Word List Reread the second paragraph on page 105. Draw a box around the word *right*. Look up the definitions of the word *right* using a dictionary. Use context clues to figure out the meaning. Write a sentence using *right* in your writer's notebook.

estimate

Shauna tried to **estimate**, or guess, the weight of her cat.

What does it mean to estimate something?

_____

_____

government

Miguel went to city hall to learn about his local **government**.

Write down one thing that your local government does.

_____

_____

independent

It's good to be **independent** and do things on your own.

How can you be more independent at home?

_____

_____

Prefixes

A prefix is a word part added to the beginning of a word. It changes the meaning of the word. The prefix _un-_ means "not." The prefix _re-_ means "again."

 FIND TEXT EVIDENCE

In the first paragraph on page 107, I see the sentence "They reread stories about candidates." _The word_ reread _has the prefix_ re-. _I know the prefix_ re- _means "again." The word_ reread _must mean "read again."_

They reread stories about candidates.

Your Turn Find the word _unsure_ on page 106. Use the prefix to figure out the meaning of the word. Write it here.

unsure _____

Reread

Stop and think about the text as you read. Do you understand what you are reading? Does it make sense? Reread to make sure you understand.

🔍 FIND TEXT EVIDENCE

Do you understand why the author thinks voting is important? Reread the first part of page 105.

Page 105

Have you ever voted? Maybe you voted to choose a class pet. Maybe your family voted on which movie to see. If you have ever voted, then you know how good it feels. Voting is important. It tells people what you think.

Many years ago, the leaders of our country wanted to know what people thought, too. They wrote a plan for our **government**. It is called the Constitution. It gives men and women in the United States the right to vote.

Each year, people who are

I read that voting is a way to tell people what you think. It is a way for people to choose new laws and leaders. Now I understand why the author thinks voting is important.

Your Turn How does Kids Voting USA teach kids to vote? Reread pages 106 and 107. Then write the answer here.

_____

_____

_____

Headings and Bar Graphs

"Every Vote Counts!" is an expository text. An **expository text**

- gives facts and information about a topic
- has headings that tell what a section is about
- includes text features, such as headings and bar graphs

FIND TEXT EVIDENCE

I can tell "Every Vote Counts!" is an expository text. It gives facts about voting. It also has headings and a bar graph.

Readers to Writers

Look at the headings in "Every Vote Counts!" Headings tell what the sections will be about. Authors use headings to organize text.

When you write, use headings to organize your topic.

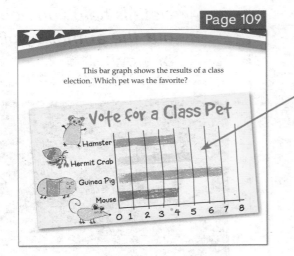

Page 109

This bar graph shows the results of a class election. Which pet was the favorite?

Vote for a Class Pet

Hamster
Hermit Crab
Guinea Pig
Mouse

0 1 2 3 4 5 6 7 8

Headings
A heading tells what a section of text is mostly about.

Bar Graph
A bar graph is a special kind of picture. It helps you understand and compare numbers and information in a quick and easy way.

Your Turn Look at the bar graph on page 109. Talk with a partner about something you learned. Write it here.

_____

_____

_____

Author's Point of View

An author's point of view is what the author thinks and feels about a topic. Look for details that show the author's thoughts and feelings. Then decide if you agree with them.

 FIND TEXT EVIDENCE

What does the author think about voting? I can reread and look for details that tell me what the author thinks. This will help me figure out the author's point of view.

Details
The title of the text is "Every Vote Counts!"
The author thinks it's sad that only six out of every ten Americans vote.
Voting gives Americans the right to choose.

↓

Point of View
Voting is important. Everyone should vote.

Details help you figure out the author's point of view.

 Your Turn Reread "Every Vote Counts!" Find details that show how the author feels about Kids Voting USA. Write the details in the graphic organizer. What is the author's point of view? Do you agree with it?

Details

↓

Author's Point of View

Respond to Reading

COLLABORATE

Talk about the prompt below. Think about different ways the author explains voting. Use your notes and graphic organizer.

How does the author help you understand that every vote counts?

_____

_____

_____

_____

_____

_____

_____

_____

Writing Correspondence

A thank-you note is a way to let people know that you are thankful for something they did. A **thank-you note**

- includes a greeting
- uses a friendly tone and shares reasons for thanking the person it's sent to
- has a closing

Think about the town where you live. Many people work hard to provide services. For example, people pick up your garbage and take care of your roads and parks. This takes a lot of work!

Look at the thank-you note below. Why is Akilah sending a note to Ms. James?

_____

_____

COLLABORATE

Write a Thank-You Note Choose a person who works in your town. Write a thank-you note. Remember to

- write reasons why you are thankful
- write in a friendly, informal tone using everyday vocabulary
- include your name

Add an illustration to your note. Share your note with a partner.

Dear Ms. James,

Thank you for taking such good care of the new baseball field at Turner Park. My friends and I like playing ball there.

Sincerely,
Akilah

*Literature Anthology:
pages 100–119*

Vote!

 How does the author help you understand that voting is important?

 Talk About It Reread page 104 and look at the illustrations. Talk with a partner about how important each person's vote is.

Cite Text Evidence What clues in the text and illustrations help you see that every vote counts? Write them in the chart.

Text Evidence	Illustration Clues	How It Helps

💡 Evaluate Information

As you read, evaluate details to identify key ideas. Ask: *What details does the author use to help me understand how she feels about voting?* Focus on clues that help you see why voting is important.

Write The author helps me understand how voting is important by

_____

_____

_____

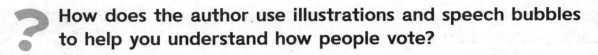

? **How does the author use illustrations and speech bubbles to help you understand how people vote?**

Talk About It Analyze the illustrations and speech bubbles on pages 112–113. Talk with a partner about what it is like to vote.

Cite Text Evidence How do the pictures and words help you understand the voting process? Write evidence in the chart.

Illustrations Show	Speech Bubbles Explain

Write Illustrations and speech bubbles help me understand _____

_____

_____

_____

_____

Quick Tip

I can use these sentence starters when we talk about how to vote.

The illustrations show...

The speech bubbles help me understand...

Make Inferences

The illustrations show curtains surrounding each voting booth. Use text evidence and make an inference, or an educated guess, to answer the question: Why do the voting booths have curtains?

? **How does the author help you understand what happens at a swearing-in ceremony?**

Talk About It Reread pages 118 and 119. Look at the illustrations. Talk about what happens during and after a swearing-in ceremony.

Cite Text Evidence What clues show what happens during and after a swearing-in ceremony? Write them here.

> **Quick Tip**
>
> When I reread, I can look for text evidence to answer questions.

> **Make Inferences**
>
> An inference is a guess based on evidence. The author says that the new mayor won't please all the people all the time. Make an inference about which group of voters is more likely to be happy with her and which is more likely to be unhappy.

Write The author helps me understand what happens by

_____

_____

_____

_____

Respond to Reading

Answer the prompt below. Think about what you learned about voting. Use your notes and graphic organizer.

How does the author help you understand how American citizens are responsible for the way our government works?

_____

_____

_____

_____

_____

_____

_____

_____

_____

_____

_____

_____

Quick Tip

Use these sentence starters to talk about how American citizens are responsible for the way our government works.

The author organizes the text by...

She includes many examples of...

That helps me understand...

Self-Selected Reading

Choose a text. Read the first two pages. If five or more words are unfamiliar, pick another text. Fill in your writer's notebook with the title, author, genre, and your purpose for reading.

A Plan for the People

Literature Anthology:
pages 122–125

A Summer of Arguments

1   The meetings began on a hot day in May 1787. The delegates gathered together in the Philadelphia State House. They closed the windows because the meetings were secret. It was hot in the State House. When they opened the windows to cool off, bugs flew in. The delegates argued all summer in the hot, buggy rooms. Making a new plan for government was not easy or fun.

2   Some delegates wanted one person to run the new government. Others thought a group should be in charge. They all agreed on one thing. A group should make laws for the country. But they disagreed on how to pick these leaders. The famous inventor and statesman Benjamin Franklin attended the meetings. He wondered how the groups could ever make any decisions.

Reread and use the prompts to take notes in the text.

Reread paragraph 1. **Underline** words that help you visualize what the Philadelphia State House was like during the meetings.

COLLABORATE

Talk with a partner about what the delegates agreed and disagreed about in paragraph 2. **Circle** the things they disagreed about.

Why is "A Summer of Arguments" a good heading for this section? Use your annotations to explain.

_____

_____

_____

_____

Making a Plan

[3] The delegates wrote their plan and called it the United States Constitution. The Constitution was only a few pages long, but it was full of big ideas. The Constitution shows how our government works. It says that people are in charge of the government. People vote to pick their leaders. These leaders run the government for the people.

A Government That's Fair to All

[4] The delegates planning the Constitution met for four months. They thought the Constitution was a good plan. But not all delegates signed it on September 15, 1787. Some of them wanted to make sure the government protected people's rights, too. A right is something you are allowed to have or do. In 1791, Congress changed the Constitution to protect the rights of American citizens. One right allows people to speak freely. These changes were called the Bill of Rights.

Underline the sentences in paragraph 3 that help you understand more about the Constitution.

COLLABORATE

Reread paragraph 4. Talk with a partner about how the author uses cause and effect to explain how the Bill of Rights was created. Remember to listen and respond to the information presented by your partner.

Circle why some delegates decided not to sign the Constitution.

What was the effect? **Draw a box around** it and write it here.

_____

_____

_____

_____

_____

_____

? How does the author use headings to help you learn how America's leaders wrote the Constitution?

Talk About It Reread the headings on pages 123 and 124. Talk with a partner about why the author uses these headings to organize the text.

Cite Text Evidence How does each heading help organize and explain the topic? Write text evidence in the web.

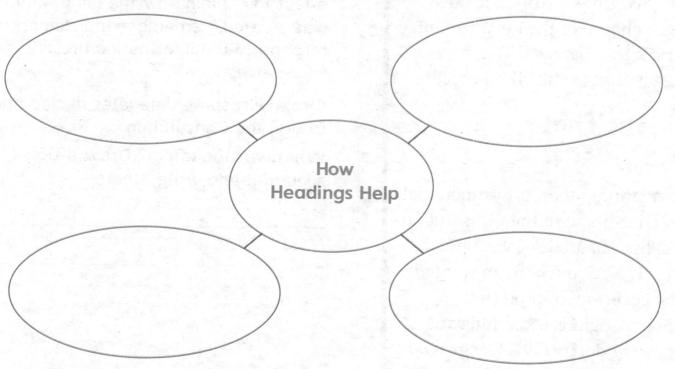

How Headings Help

Write The author uses headings to help me understand _____

_____

_____

Author's Purpose

Writers have a purpose, or reason, for writing. They can write to inform, entertain, or persuade. Choosing the right text structure, or way to organize text, helps them achieve their purpose.

FIND TEXT EVIDENCE

In the last paragraph of page 122, the author uses a compare-and-contrast text structure to help readers understand the different sides of an important debate about our government.

> Some delegates wanted one person to run the new government. Others thought a group should be in charge. They all agreed on one thing. A group should make laws for the country. But they disagreed on how to pick these leaders.

Your Turn Reread paragraph 4 on page 123.

- How does the author use text structure to help you understand why we have a Bill of Rights? _____

_____

_____

_____

Text Connections

? **How does the information you read in *Vote!* and "A Plan for the People" help you understand what is happening in the engraving?**

Talk About It With a partner, discuss what you see in the engraving. Read the caption and talk about what happened to make the event shown in the engraving possible.

Cite Text Evidence Reread the caption. **Underline** evidence that explains how people make government work. **Circle** one clue in the engraving that shows George Washington is taking the oath of office.

Write The information in "Vote!" and "A Plan for the People" helps me understand more about what is happening in the engraving by _____

_____

_____

_____

_____

Time & Life Pictures/The LIFE Picture Collection/Getty Images

WASHINGTON TAKING THE OATH AS PRESIDENT, APRIL 30, 1789, ON THE SITE OF THE PRESENT TREASURY BUILDING, WALL STREET, NEW YORK CITY.

This engraving shows George Washington taking the oath of office on April 30, 1789. Americans voted for Washington and on this day, he was sworn in as their president.

Present Your Work

COLLABORATE

Decide how you will present your thank-you note to the class. Use the presenting checklist as you practice your presentation. Discuss the sentence starters below and write your answers.

Quick Tip

Think about reading your thank-you note as if the person it's for is standing right in front of you. Be prepared to answer questions about what you are saying thank you for.

An interesting thing I learned about my town is _____

_____

I think my presentation was _____

I know because _____

_____

_____

_____

✓ **Presenting Checklist**

☐ I will practice reading my note.

☐ I will look at the audience.

☐ I will speak clearly and slowly.

☐ I will listen carefully to questions from the audience.

Literature Anthology:
pages 100–101

Expert Model

Features of Expository Essay

An **expository essay** is a form of expository text. It presents ideas and information about a topic. An expository essay

- has an introduction that makes the reader want to keep reading
- presents facts, details, and information in a logical order
- provides a conclusion that relates to the topic

Word Wise

Writers use different kinds of nouns when they write. These words include common nouns, such as *election* and *winner*, and proper nouns, such as *Election Day* and *Mayor Smith*. Proper nouns begin with capital letters.

Analyze an Expert Model Reread pages 102 and 103 of *Vote!* in the **Literature Anthology**. Use evidence from the bubbles and illustrations to answer the questions.

How does the author introduce her topic in a way that makes you want to keep reading? _____

_____

_____

How does the author help you understand how candidates convince people to vote for them? _____

_____

_____

Plan: Choose Your Topic

Brainstorm With a partner, brainstorm a list of things you learned about voting and how people make government work. Use the sentence starters below to talk about your ideas.

I read about . . .

This is interesting to me because . . .

Writing Prompt Choose one of the ideas from your list. Write an essay explaining your topic.

I will write about _____

Purpose and Audience An author's purpose is the main reason for writing. Your audience is who will be reading the work.

The reason I chose this topic is _____

_____

I want my audience to _____

_____

Plan In your writer's notebook, make a Word Web to plan your writing. In the center write your topic.

Quick Tip

When a writer wants to share information with readers, he or she writes an essay. When you are choosing your topic, think about what is interesting to you. That will make your essay more fun to write and more fun for your readers to read.

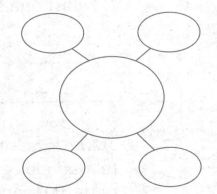

Plan: Research

Paraphrase Research your topic using a variety of source materials. As you take notes, remember to paraphrase, or write the meaning of the text in your own words. Record the author, title, and publication information for each source for your works cited page. Here's an example of how to list this information.

> Smith, Jane. *How Government Works*. Houston. Checkers
> Press. 2017. Print

Notice how the author's name is written. **Circle** the author's last name. The title is in italics. **Underline** the name of the article or book.

Now list one source you will use. Follow the model above.

_____

_____

 Take Notes In your writer's notebook, take notes by adding related ideas and details to your Word Web. Create a works cited page. Put your list of sources in alphabetical order.

Digital Tools

For more information on how to cite sources, watch "Cite Your Sources." Read the "Sample Works Cited Page." Go to **my.mheducation. com.**

Draft

Developing the Topic Authors use relevant details to develop their topic into an engaging essay. The author of "Every Vote Counts!" grabs your attention with a question, then gives details.

> Did you know that only about six out of every ten Americans vote?
> That's sad. Some people think that voting is too hard. They are unsure
> of where to go to vote. They think it takes too much time. Now, a
> group called Kids Voting USA is trying to convince everyone to vote.

Use the above paragraph as a model to start writing your essay. Think of a way to get readers to want to keep reading. Use relevant details to support your ideas.

_____

_____

_____

_____

 Write a Draft Use your Word Web to write your draft in your writer's notebook. Remember that a strong beginning will make readers want to keep reading.

Revise

Strong Conclusion An expository essay needs a strong conclusion that stresses its most important points. The conclusion should repeat the main idea of the essay in a new way.

Reread the last paragraph from "Every Vote Counts!" on page 108. Talk with a partner about how the author ends the essay. Write about it.

_____

_____

_____

Revise It's time to revise your writing. Read your draft and look for places where you might

- add more details that support the topic

- make your conclusion stronger

Circle two sentences in your draft that you can change. Revise and write them here.

_____

_____

_____

Peer Conferences

Review a Draft Listen carefully as a partner reads his or her draft aloud. Say what you like about the draft. Use these sentence starters to help discuss your partner's draft.

I like this part because it helped me understand . . .

This part is unclear to me. Can you explain why . . .

I have a question about . . .

Partner Feedback After you take turns giving each other feedback, write one suggestion from your partner that you will use in your revision.

_____

_____

_____

_____

_____

Revision Use the Revising Checklist to figure out what you can change to make your expository essay better. Remember to use the rubric on page 135 to help with your revision.

✔ Revising Checklist

☐ Does my introduction make readers want to keep reading?

☐ Did I include facts and details that explain my topic?

☐ Are my facts and details in a logical order?

☐ Does my essay end with a strong conclusion?

Edit and Proofread

After you revise your expository essay, proofread it to find any mistakes in grammar, spelling, and punctuation. Read your draft at least three times. This will help you catch any mistakes. Use the checklist below to edit your sentences.

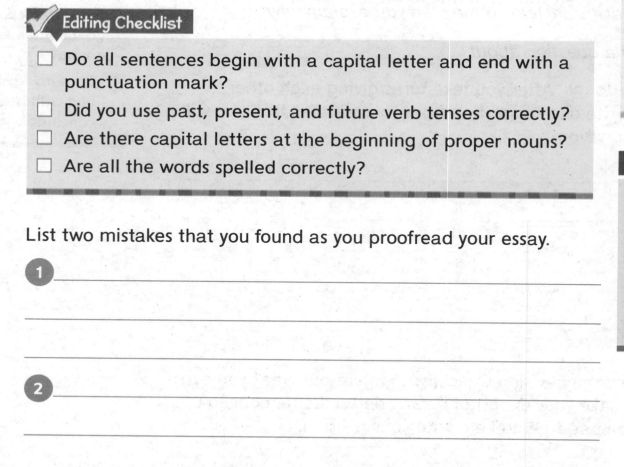

✓ Editing Checklist

- ☐ Do all sentences begin with a capital letter and end with a punctuation mark?
- ☐ Did you use past, present, and future verb tenses correctly?
- ☐ Are there capital letters at the beginning of proper nouns?
- ☐ Are all the words spelled correctly?

List two mistakes that you found as you proofread your essay.

1 _____

_____

_____

2 _____

_____

_____

! Tech Tip

If you wrote your draft on a computer, use the spell-check feature to find spelling mistakes. This feature will also suggest correct spellings. The spell-check might not find every misspelled word though, so proofread your draft as well.

Grammar Connections

When you proofread your draft for punctuation mistakes, remember to use end punctuation that fits the kind of sentences you wrote.

Publish, Present, and Evaluate

Publishing When you publish your writing, you create a neat final copy that is free of mistakes. If you are not using a computer, write neatly. Leave the space of a pencil point between letters and the space of a pencil eraser between words.

Presentation When you are ready to present, practice your presentation. Use the presenting checklist.

Evaluate After you publish, use the rubric to evaluate your essay.

✔ Presenting Checklist

☐ Look at the audience.

☐ Speak slowly and clearly.

☐ Communicate your main ideas effectively.

☐ Hold any visual aids so that everyone can see them.

What did you do successfully? _____

_____

What needs more work? _____

_____

4	3	2	1
• includes a strong introduction • includes many relevant details in a logical order • includes a strong conclusion that sums up the topic	• includes an interesting introduction • includes some details in a logical order • includes a conclusion with a detail related to the topic	• introduction is unclear • very few facts and details related to the topic • conclusion does not inform readers or sum up topic	• no introduction • does not focus on a particular topic • no relevant facts or details

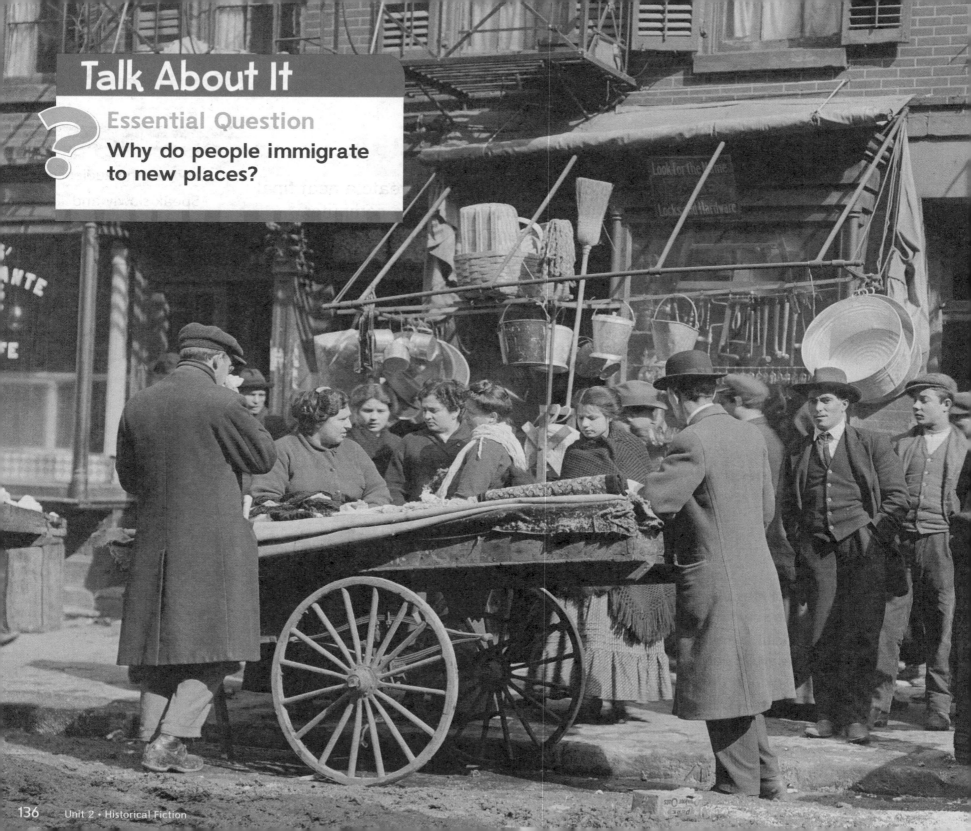

Talk About It

COLLABORATE

This is Hester Street. Many immigrants moved here and worked on this New York City street. They came for many reasons. Immigrants dreamed about new jobs. They felt there were lots of opportunities. They believed their lives would be better.

Look at the photograph. What is immigration? Write what you have learned in the word web.

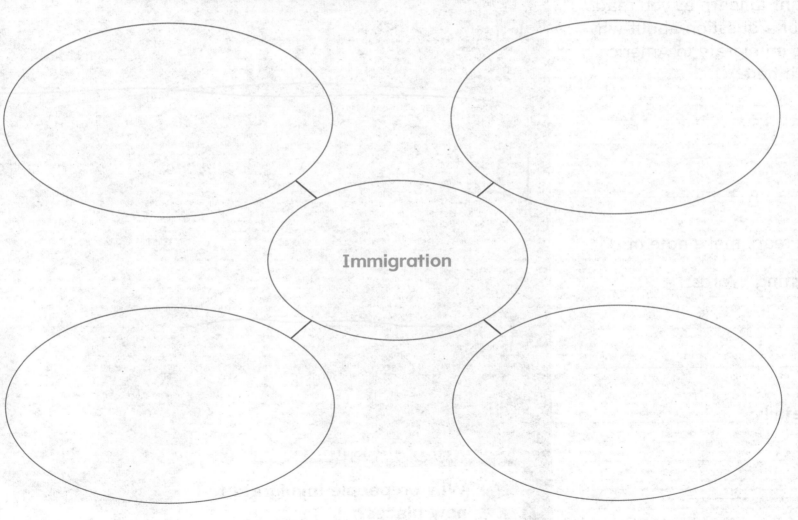

Immigration

BLAST BACK!
studysync

Go online to **my.mheducation.com** and read the "Leaving Home" Blast. Think about how geography can influence immigration. Then blast back your response.

Historical Fiction

TAKE NOTES

Asking questions before you read helps you figure out what you want to learn as you read. Think of a question about why people immigrate to America. Write it here.

_____

_____

_____

As you read, make note of:

Interesting Words: _____

_____

_____

Key Details: _____

_____

_____

_____

SAILING TO AMERICA

Essential Question

? Why do people immigrate to new places?

Read about why one family came to America.

Nora woke early. She hadn't slept much. It was March, 1895. Da was leaving for America today. Uncle Sean **immigrated** there last year and found work right away. He asked Da to join him. It was Mama and Da's dream to one day live in America.

Nora lit a lamp for light and sat down at the table. Her brother, Danny, joined her.

"I feel like crying," he **whispered** softly.

"I know," Nora answered. "So do I, but this is Da and Mama's dream. Da will find work and send for us. Look at the **photographs** that Uncle Sean sent. Doesn't America look grand?"

Tristan Elwell

FIND TEXT EVIDENCE

Read

Paragraph 1

Theme

What happened to Uncle Sean when he got to America?

_____

_____

Circle text evidence.

Paragraphs 2–4

Make Predictions

Underline how Nora and Danny feel about moving to America. What will Nora do to make Danny feel better?

_____

_____

Reread

Author's Craft

How does the author help you understand that Nora and her family lived a long time ago?

Paragraph 1
Theme
Circle two reasons Danny doesn't want to go to America.

Paragraphs 2–3
Make Predictions
Review the prediction you made on page 139. **Underline** clues that confirm it. Correct your prediction if it was wrong.

Paragraph 3
Events
What is Da going to do?

Draw a box around text evidence.

Reread
Author's Craft

How does the author use dialogue to help you understand how Danny and Nora feel about moving?

4 "I don't want to ever leave Ireland," Danny said. "We won't have any friends in America. We'll be far away from Grandda, Paddy, and Colleen."

5 "Maybe you'll be glad it isn't Ireland," Nora said. "There will be enough food to eat. Mama and Da can relax and not worry so much. We'll all have a better life. America will be the land of our dreams."

6 Then Da carried a bag into the room. "Cheer up, my little loves! Why, in no time at all, you'll be joining me."

A year later, Da had saved enough money to send for his family. Mama, Danny, and Nora packed what little they had. They got on a crowded steamship and began their voyage.

The trip across the Atlantic Ocean was rough. The air inside the steamship smelled like a dirty sock. The ship tossed up and down for days. The waves were as big as mountains. Many passengers became seasick, but Nora and Danny felt fine.

Every day Nora daydreamed and reread Da's letters. She thought of the buildings and streetcars he wrote about. In her dreams, she could picture Da on a crowded street. He had a big smile on his face.

Tristan Elwell

FIND TEXT EVIDENCE

Read

Paragraphs 1-2
Make Predictions
Draw a box around one detail about the steamship. What will the trip be like?

_____

_____

Read paragraph 2. Confirm or revise your prediction.

Paragraph 3
Theme
What does Nora do every day? **Underline** text evidence.

Reread
Author's Craft

How does the illustration help you understand how Nora feels?

FIND TEXT EVIDENCE

Read

Paragraph 1
Make Predictions
What do you predict is happening as Nora wakes up?

_____

_____

Draw a box around clues.

Paragraph 2
Similes
Underline a sentence that compares two things. What does it compare?

_____

_____

Paragraph 3
Theme
Write how the people feel when they arrive in America.

_____

_____

Circle text evidence.

One morning, Nora awoke. A **moment** later, she realized something was different. The ocean was as smooth as glass.

A few hours later, Nora, Danny, and Mama shivered together on the ship's deck. Snowflakes drifted through the air. Another traveler noticed and gave them a blanket. It was as thin as a rag, but nothing could have been more **valuable** to them.

Suddenly, someone shouted, "There's Lady Liberty!" As the ship passed the large statue, the crowd cheered. Someone shouted, "At last, we've **arrived**! We are in America." Soon, everyone was singing and dancing.

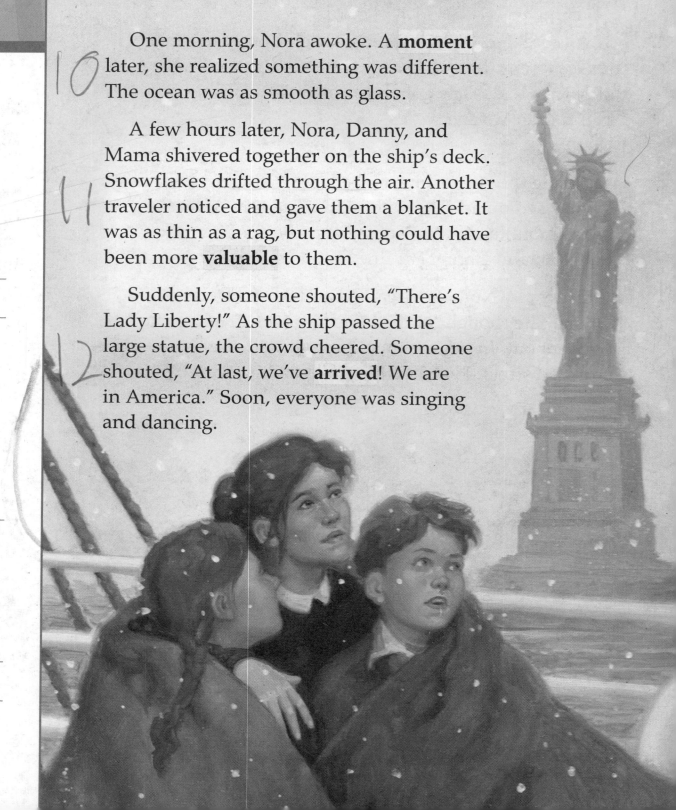

A ferry took the travelers to Ellis Island. In the main hall, doctors **inspected** the family. They looked for signs of illness. Mama had to answer many questions. Nora knew that people didn't get an **opportunity**, or chance, to take these tests twice. Nora looked at Danny, then at Mama. They had to pass.

Difficult

13

After a few hours, the family learned they could stay in America. As they filed off the ferry, Nora saw Uncle Sean's dark hair. Then she saw Da. His hands waved wildly. He had a big smile on his face. Dreams do come true, Nora thought as she waved back.

14

Summarize

Use your notes and think about what happens in "Sailing to America." Summarize the important events.

Tristan Elwell

FIND TEXT EVIDENCE

Read

Paragraph 1
Events
How did Mama, Nora, and Danny get to Ellis Island?

Underline details that tell what happened there.

Paragraph 2
Theme
Circle details that tell what Da does when he sees Nora.

Reread
Author's Craft

How does the author help you understand how Nora feels at Ellis Island?

Fluency

Take turns reading the first paragraph. Talk about how the author helps you read with feeling.

Vocabulary

Use the sentences to talk with a partner about each word. Then answer the questions.

arrived

I rang the doorbell when I **arrived** at my friend's house.

What do you do after you have arrived at school?

_____

_____

immigrated

Many people **immigrated** to the United States from other countries.

Why have some people immigrated to America?

_____

_____

inspected

Dad carefully **inspected** the tire to find out where the hole was.

What is something that you have inspected carefully?

_____

_____

moment

The bee landed on the flower for a **moment** and then flew away.

What can you do that lasts only a moment?

_____

_____

opportunity

Our class had an **opportunity**, or chance, to visit the science museum.

What is another word for opportunity?

_____

_____

 Build Your Word List Pick one of the interesting words you listed on page 138. Use a print or online dictionary to find the word's meaning. Then use the word in a sentence.

photographs

Looking at old **photographs** reminds me of things I've forgotten.

What can you learn from family photographs?

_____

_____

valuable

The card I made is very **valuable** to my grandmother.

Describe something that is valuable to you.

_____

_____

whispered

Kara **whispered** in Sofia's ear so no one else would hear her secret.

What is the opposite of whispered?

_____

_____

Similes

A simile compares two very different things. It uses the word _like_ or _as_. One example is: _Her cheeks were like red roses._

🔍 **FIND TEXT EVIDENCE**

In "Sailing to America," I see the simile, "The waves were as big as mountains." Comparing waves to mountains makes the waves seem huge and tall.

The waves were as big as mountains.

Your Turn Explain the meaning of the simile _"The air inside the steamship smelled like a dirty sock"_ from page 141.

_____

_____

_____

Tristan Elwell

Make Predictions

Use story clues to predict what happens next. Was your prediction right? Reread to confirm, or check, it. Change it if it isn't right.

 FIND TEXT EVIDENCE

What will Da do after he reaches America? You may have predicted that he would send for his family. Reread pages 140 and 141 for clues to support your prediction.

Page 140

> "I don't want to ever leave Ireland," Danny said. "We won't have any friends in America. We'll be far away from Grandda, Paddy, and Colleen."
>
> "Maybe you'll be glad it isn't Ireland," Nora said. "There will be enough food to eat. Mama and Da can relax and not worry so much. We'll all have a better life. America will be the land of our dreams."
>
> Then Da carried a bag into the room. "Cheer up, my little loves! Why, in no time at all, you'll be joining me."

I predicted that Da would bring his family to America. Here is the clue. Da says they will be joining him. I read page 141 to check it. "A year later, Da saved enough money to send for his family."

 Your Turn Predict what will happen when the family arrives in America. Find clues to support your prediction. Write your prediction here.

_____

_____

Quick Tip

A story's setting can offer clues about what will happen next. For example, you can use the change of setting from Ireland to America to predict what characters in "Sailing to America" will do.

Events and Illustrations

"Sailing to America" is historical fiction. **Historical fiction**

- is a made-up story that takes place in the past
- has illustrations that show historical details

FIND TEXT EVIDENCE

I can tell that "Sailing to America" is historical fiction. The characters and story are made up, but they are based on real events that happened a long time ago.

Page 139

Nora woke early. She hadn't slept much. It was March, 1895. Da was leaving for America today. Uncle Sean **immigrated** there last year and found work right away. He asked Da to join him. It was Mama and Da's dream to one day live in America.

Nora lit a lamp for light and sat down at the table. Her brother, Danny, joined her.

"I feel like crying," he **whispered** softly.

"I know," Nora answered. "So do I, but this is Da and Mama's dream. Da will find work and send for us. Look at the **photographs** that Uncle Sean sent. Doesn't America look grand?"

Events

The story and characters are made-up, but the events could have happened in real life. Events in historical fiction happened a long time ago.

Illustrations

Illustrations show details about how people lived.

Your Turn Find two things in "Sailing to America" that could happen in real life. Talk about why the story is historical fiction. Write your answer below.

_____

_____

_____

Tristan Elwell

Theme

The theme of a story is the author's message. To figure out the theme, notice what the characters do and say. Then, think about what deeper ideas these key details suggest.

A theme is different from a topic. A topic is what the story is about. For example, the topic of "Sailing to America" is immigration during the late 1800s.

FIND TEXT EVIDENCE

In "Sailing to America," Mama and Da dream of living in America. I think this is an important detail. I will reread to find more key details. Then I can figure out the story's theme.

```
┌─────────────────────────────┐
│           Detail            │
│  It's Mama and Da's dream to │
│      live in America.       │
└─────────────────────────────┘
              │
              ▼
┌─────────────────────────────┐
│           Detail            │
│ Danny is upset about leaving │
│          Ireland.           │
└─────────────────────────────┘
              │
              ▼
┌─────────────────────────────┐
│           Theme             │
│                             │
│                             │
└─────────────────────────────┘
```

Details tell what the characters do and say. They help you figure out the theme.

 Your Turn Reread "Sailing to America." Find more important details and write them in your graphic organizer. Use the details above and the ones you wrote to figure out the theme.

Triston Elwell

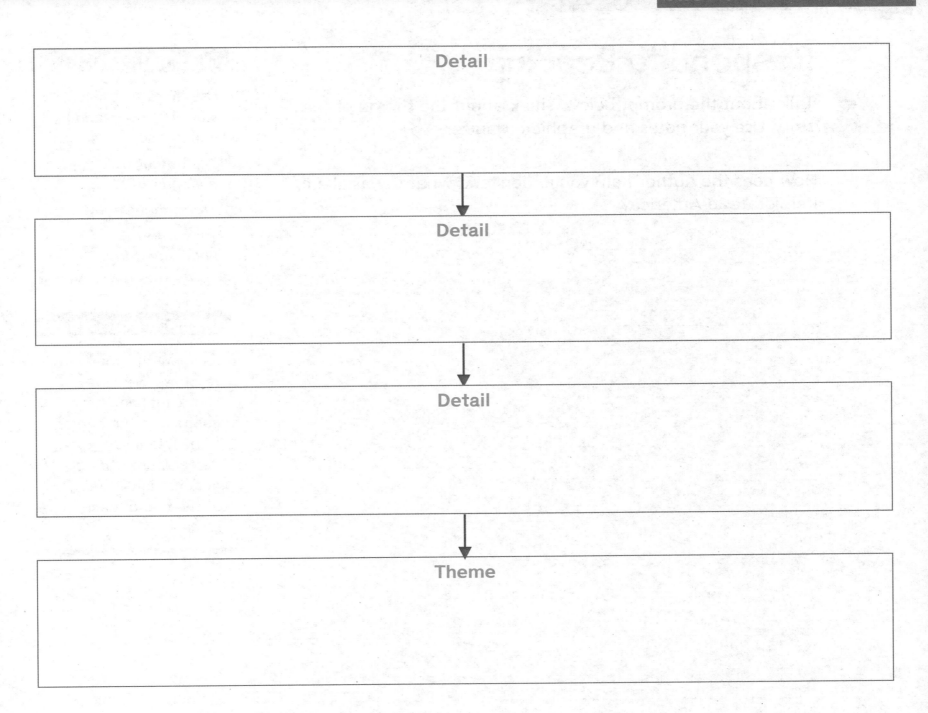

Detail

Detail

Detail

Theme

Respond to Reading

Talk about the prompt below. Think about the theme of the story. Use your notes and graphic organizer.

How does the author help you understand what it was like to immigrate to America?

_____

_____

_____

_____

_____

_____

_____

_____

_____

_____

_____

_____

Primary and Secondary Sources

Quick Tip

Relevant information includes facts and details that are related to your topic. Use a variety of sources, such as encyclopedias, photographs, and websites as you identify and gather relevant information.

Primary sources help us learn about the past. A primary source may be an original document or something written by someone who took part in an event. Photographs from the past, letters, and diary entries are examples of primary sources.

Secondary sources are created by someone who was not at an event. Encyclopedias and textbooks are examples of secondary sources.

Look at the illustration below. Are the examples pictured primary or secondary sources? Explain why.

Write a Journal Entry Pretend you are an immigrant traveling with your family to America in the 1800s. Write a journal entry about it.

1. Identify and gather relevant information. Use at least one primary source.

2. Write your journal entry.

3. Share your entry with a partner.

The Castle on Hester Street

 How does the author use dialogue to help you get to know what Julie's grandparents are like?

Literature Anthology: pages 126–141

 Talk About It Reread pages 130 and 131. Discuss with a partner how Julie's grandmother reacts to Sol's story.

Cite Text Evidence What clues in the dialogue help you get to know Julie's grandparents? Write text evidence in the diagram.

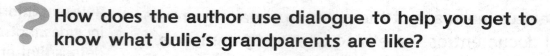

Make Inferences

An inference is a guess based on evidence and what you already know. What inference can you make about Grandfather based on the story he tells Julie?

What Do the Characters Say?	What Does It Mean?

Write The author uses dialogue to _____

_____

_____

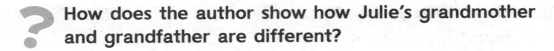

? **How does the author show how Julie's grandmother and grandfather are different?**

COLLABORATE

Talk About It Reread page 132. Talk with a partner about Julie's grandmother's version of their trip to America.

Cite Text Evidence Now reread the last paragraph on page 133. What clues help you see how different Julie's grandparents are?

Julie's Grandmother	Julie's Grandfather	How They Are Different

Write I know Julie's grandparents are different because the author

_____

_____

Quick Tip

I can use these sentence starters when we talk about Julie's grandparents.

The author uses Julie's grandparents' stories to ...

This helps me understand ...

Evaluate Information

Think about the story Julie's grandmother tells and the effect it has on both Julie and her grandfather. Talk about why Julie's grandfather makes up stories rather than tells what really happened.

? **How do the illustrations help you understand how Julie's grandparents felt about living in America?**

Talk About It Look at the illustrations on pages 136 and 137. Turn to a partner and talk about what they show.

Cite Text Evidence What clues in the illustrations show how Julie's grandparents feel about living in America? Write clues in the chart.

How Do Julie's Grandparents Feel?	
Clues on page 136	Clues on page 137
What They Mean	What They Mean

Write The illustrations help me understand _____

_____

_____

Respond to Reading

COLLABORATE

Answer the prompt below. Think about how the author shows the differences between Julie's grandmother and grandfather. Use your notes and graphic organizer.

How does Linda Heller use the stories Julie's grandparents tell to help you compare how they felt about coming to America?

_____

_____

_____

_____

_____

_____

_____

_____

_____

_____

Quick Tip

Use these sentence starters to talk about Julie's grandparents.

Julie's grandfather's stories are ...

Linda Heller tells the grandmother's point of view to show ...

This helps me see that they ...

Self-Selected Reading

Choose a text. In your writer's notebook, write the title, author, and genre of the book. As you read, make a connection to ideas in other texts you have read or to a personal experience. Write your ideas in your notebook.

Next Stop, America!

Literature Anthology:
pages 144–147

What Happened at Ellis Island

1 Immigrants crossed the ocean on crowded ships. When the ships arrived in New York harbor, smaller boats took them to Ellis Island. There the travelers hoped to become American citizens. Thousands of people came every day.

2 First, everyone had to have a check-up. The government didn't want sick people coming into the country. As a result, some sick people stayed in the Ellis Island hospital until they were well. Someone with an eye infection was sent back across the ocean!

3 People also had to take a written test. They had to answer questions, give their names, and tell what country they were from. They had to tell where they planned to go. They had to promise to obey the laws of the United States.

4 After hours of waiting, most people got good news. The United States welcomed them to their new home.

Reread and use the prompts to take notes in the text.

In paragraph 1, **circle** how many people came to Ellis Island every day.

Reread paragraphs 2–4. **Write numbers next to** the sentences that describe what immigrants had to do at Ellis Island.

COLLABORATE

Reread paragraph 4. Talk with a partner about how immigrants felt about being allowed to stay in America. How many got to stay? **Underline** text that answers the question. Write it here.

_____

_____

_____

Where They Went

[5]   From Ellis Island, some immigrants got on ferries to New York City. Many people's journeys ended there. Thousands settled near friends and family. They stayed in neighborhoods, such as Little Italy and the Lower East Side. Others had more traveling to do. They headed west or south, to other cities and states. Some went to places where they could get a job in a factory or a mine. Others found good farmland. No matter where the immigrants settled, they never forgot Ellis Island.

Reread the excerpt. **Underline** the sentence that helps you understand that most of the immigrants stayed in New York. Write it here:

_____

_____

Circle the places where they settled.

Talk with a partner about why Ellis Island was a memorable place for immigrants.

Draw a box around the text evidence that supports your discussion.

Bettmann/Getty Images

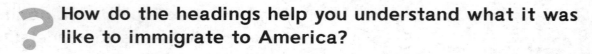

? **How do the headings help you understand what it was like to immigrate to America?**

Talk About It Reread the excerpts on pages 156 and 157. Talk about why "What Happened at Ellis Island" is a good heading.

Cite Text Evidence What clues in the headings and photograph help you understand the text better? Write them in the chart.

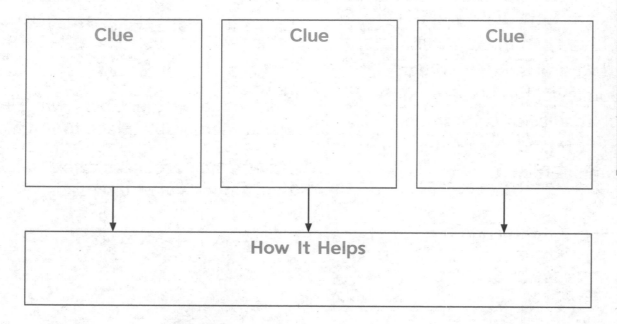

Clue	Clue	Clue

How It Helps

Write The author uses headings to _____

_____

_____

Quick Tip

In an informational text, or text meant to inform readers, authors often use headings and photographs to support understanding. Headings help identify the main topic of each section. Photographs illustrate key details in the text. Look at the photograph on page 157. Think about how it connects to the text.

Cause and Effect

A cause is why something happens. An effect is what happens. Cause and effect happen in time order. Words such as *because* and *as a result* signal cause and effect.

FIND TEXT EVIDENCE

*On page 145 of "Next Stop, America!" in the **Literature Anthology** I read that many immigrants came to America. This is the effect. I can use the signal word because to find the cause. Immigrants wanted the right to live and speak as they wished. That's why they came.*

They came to America because they wanted the right to live and speak as they wished.

Your Turn Reread the second paragraph on page 156.

- How does the author help you figure out what the effect is?

_____

_____

- How do you know what the cause is?_____

_____

_____

Readers to Writers

Writers use organizational patterns such as cause and effect when they write informational text. Signal words such as *because* and *as a result* help readers figure out why events happen. When you write, use signal words to help your readers find causes and effects. This helps them understand your topic better.

Text Connections

? How do the *The Castle on Hester Street,* "Next Stop, America!," and the photograph below help you understand why people came to America?

Talk About It Read the caption and look at the photograph. Talk with a partner about what you notice. Choose one person in the photo and describe what he is doing.

Cite Text Evidence **Circle** three clues in the photograph that help you understand what the boys are doing. **Underline** words and phrases in the caption that give more information about why immigrants come to America.

Write The photograph, *The Castle on Hester Street,* and "Next Stop, America!" help me understand that people came to America to

_____

_____

_____

_____

_____

_____

Quick Tip

The photographer helps me understand how hard immigrants had to work. This helps me compare the texts with the photograph.

This photograph was taken in 1909 by photographer Lewis Wickes Hine. It is called "Immigrants in Night School" and shows a classroom in Boston, Massachusetts.

Integrate | RESEARCH AND INQUIRY

Present Your Work

COLLABORATE

Decide how you will present your journal entry to the class. Make a clean copy of your work. Use the checklist to improve your presentation.

September 5, 1889
I arrived in New York Harbor today.

I saw the Statue of Liberty!

Before I present, I will figure out how to express what it feels like to immigrate to America by:

_____

I think my presentation was _____

I know because _____

_____

Tech Tip

Record yourself reading your journal entry, then listen to the recording. Did you speak loudly enough for your audience to hear you? Did you speak clearly and at an appropriate speed? Practice reading your journal entry out loud several times.

✔ Presenting Checklist

☐ I will practice my presentation.

☐ I will speak clearly and slowly.

☐ I will speak loudly enough for all to hear.

☐ I will use my voice to express how I would feel if I immigrated to America.

 Essential Question

How do people figure things out?

When I go biking with my family, it's my job to figure out where to go. I use a map and ask questions to find the best places to ride. Then my family and I discuss our choices and decide together.

Look at the photograph. Talk about how you decide what to do. Write about how you figure things out in the graphic organizer.

Figure It Out

Go online to **my.mheducation.com** and read the "I Spy with My Little Eye" Blast. Think about why observation plays an important role in science. Then blast back your response.

TAKE NOTES

Understanding why you are reading helps you adjust how you read. Preview the poems and establish a purpose for reading. Write it here.

_____

_____

_____

_____

As you read, make note of:

Interesting Words:

_____

_____

_____

Key Details:

_____

_____

_____

Empanada Day

One bite of Abuelita's empanadas
And my mouth purrs like a cat.
"Teach me," I beg and bounce on my feet,
"Teach me to make this magical treat."
Abuelita smiles,
"Be an observer, watch and learn,
Then you too can take a turn."

Essential Question

? **How do people figure things out?**

Read poems about different ways to figure things out.

(handwritten notes: "empanadas George", "important to teach how to make them?")

Dara Goldman

She sets before me a ball of dough,
Round and golden as the sun.
My eyes wide as saucers, I watch and follow,

Press circles flat as pancakes,
Spoon on apple slices and nose-tickling spices,
Seal it all in, a half-moon envelope of bliss.
Together we write down every step
As the empanadas bake and crisp in the oven,
My stomach rumbling like a hungry bear.

Ah, empanada day!

— George Santiago

POETRY

FIND TEXT EVIDENCE

Read

Page 164
Alliteration
Put a box around words in the last line that start with the same sound.

Page 165
Simile
A simile uses the word *like* or *as* to compare two different things. **Circle** the similes. Pick one and write what it compares.

_____

_____

Pages 164–165
Point of View
Who is the narrator of this poem? _____

Reread

Author's Craft

How does the poet help you understand how empanadas are made?

FIND TEXT EVIDENCE

Read

Page 166

Rhyme

Underline three words that rhyme in "Cold Feet."

Page 166

Alliteration

Draw a box around two words that start with the same sound in "Our Washing Machine."

Page 166

Point of View

What does the narrator think about the washing machine?

_____

_____

Circle text evidence.

Reread

Author's Craft

In "Cold Feet," how does the poet help you visualize the inventor's problem?

Cold Feet

An inventor with feet like ice,

And toes like ten shivering mice,

Looked at clothes, studied feet.

Read about cold and heat,

And knit the first socks, warm and nice.

OUR WASHING MACHINE

Our washing machine is a bear

That munches up socks by the pair.

He will suds them and grumble

As they spin, turn, and tumble,

Then spit them out, ready to wear.

Dara Goldman

Bugged

A creature has crawled on my knee,

It's a bug green and round as a pea.

His five wings are fish fins,

He's got teeth sharp as pins.

Just imagine him chomping on me!

I read every bug book I see,

To learn what this creature might be.

I ask scientists too,

But they don't have a clue.

So I'm **bugged** by this great mystery.

Make Connections

What do all four poems have in common? Use your notes to talk about how they are alike.

FIND TEXT EVIDENCE

Read

Stanza 1
Point of View
How does the narrator feel about the creature?

_____

_____

Underline text evidence.

Stanza 2
Rhyme
Circle three words that rhyme. Now find two more words that rhyme. Write them here.

_____

_____

Reread

Author's Craft

Why is "Bugged" a good title for this poem?

Vocabulary

Use the sentences to talk with a partner about each word. Then answer the questions.

bounce

Keith likes to **bounce** a soccer ball off his head.

How many times can you bounce a ball ?

_____

_____

imagine

Mandy likes to **imagine** what it was like to live 100 years ago.

What do you like to imagine?

_____

_____

inventor

Thomas Edison is the **inventor** of the first light bulb.

What does an inventor do?

_____

_____

observer

Gina is a good **observer** and enjoys watching birds.

Write about a time when you were an observer at an event.

_____

_____

Poetry Words

alliteration

"Poets paint precise pictures" is an example of **alliteration**.

Give another example of alliteration.

_____

_____

free verse

Jeremy likes to write **free verse** poems because they don't need to rhyme.

What would you write a free verse poem about?

_____

_____

limerick

Hana's **limerick** had five lines and made the class laugh.

How is a limerick different from other poems?

_____

_____

rhyme

The words *cat* and *bat* **rhyme** because they end in the same sound.

Name two other words that rhyme.

_____

_____

Build Your Word List Reread the last line of "Empanada Day" on page 165. **Underline** the word *rumbling*. Draw a Word Web in your writer's notebook. Write the word *rumbling* in the center. Then, use a dictionary to fill in other forms of the word.

Simile

A simile uses the word *like* or *as* to compare two things that are very different. An example of a simile is, "The moon is like a giant pearl."

FIND TEXT EVIDENCE

To find a simile, I need to look for two things that are being compared. In "Cold Feet," I see the line, "An inventor with feet like ice." The simile compares the inventor's feet with ice. That means her feet were very cold.

An inventor with feet like ice,

Your Turn Reread "Cold Feet" on page 166. Find another simile and write it below. Then write what the simile compares and what it means.

_____

_____

Dara Goldman

Alliteration and Rhyme

Poets use alliteration and rhyme to draw attention to certain words and to make poems sound musical.

Alliteration is the use of words that start with the same sound. **Rhyme** is when words end in the same sound.

 FIND TEXT EVIDENCE

Read aloud the poem "Bugged" on page 167. Listen for beginning sounds that repeat. Listen for words that rhyme.

Quick Tip

Words that rhyme might not look alike. *Pea* and *knee* end in the same sound, but the sound is spelled differently. It is helpful to read the poem aloud to find all the rhymes.

Page 167

Bugged

A creature has crawled on my knee,
It's a bug green and round as a pea.
His five wings are fish fins,
He's got teeth sharp as pins.
Just imagine him chomping on me!

I read every bug book I see,
To learn what this creature might be.
I ask scientists too,
But they don't have a clue.
So I'm **bugged** by this great mystery.

In the first line, the words crawled *and* creature *start with the same sound.*

The words knee *and* pea *rhyme. I like the way these words sound.*

Your Turn Reread "Bugged." Write two more examples of alliteration here.

_____

_____

Limerick and Free Verse

A **limerick** is a short funny poem that rhymes. Each stanza has five lines. The first, second, and fifth lines rhyme. The third and fourth lines rhyme. This is called the poem's rhyme scheme.

Free Verse does not always rhyme. It can have any number of lines and stanzas.

FIND TEXT EVIDENCE

I can tell that "Cold Feet" is a limerick. It is funny. The stanza has five lines. Some of the lines rhyme.

A limerick has a rhyme scheme, or pattern of rhyme, that makes it sound funny. A free verse poem can be funny or serious.

When writing a poem, try starting with a freewrite to find what you want to say. Then, pick the genre that best fits your purpose.

Page 166

Cold Feet

An inventor with feet like ice,
And toes like ten shivering mice,
Looked at clothes, studied feet.
Read about cold and heat,
And knit the first socks, warm and nice.

OUR WASHING MACHINE

Our washing machine is a bear
That munches up socks by the pair.
He will suds them and grumble
As they spin, turn, and tumble,
Then spit them out, ready to wear.

In this funny limerick, the first, second, and fifth lines rhyme. This limerick has one stanza. A stanza is a group of lines in a poem.

Your Turn Reread the poems "Our Washing Machine" and "Empanada Day." Explain whether each poem is free verse or a limerick. Write your answer below.

COLLABORATE

_____

_____

_____

_____

Point of View

A poem often shows a narrator's thoughts about events or characters. This is the point of view. Look for details that show point of view.

🔍 **FIND TEXT EVIDENCE**

I'll read "Empanada Day" and look for details that show what the narrator thinks about making empanadas with Abuelita, his grandmother. This is his point of view.

Quick Tip

The narrator of "Empanada Day" uses the pronouns *I*, *me*, or *my*. That means the poem is told by a first-person narrator. Who is narrating "Bugged"?

Details
One bite of Abuelita's empanadas and my mouth purrs.
Teach me to make this magical treat.
My eyes wide as saucers, I watch and follow.

↓

Point of View

 Your Turn Reread "Empanada Day." Write more details and the narrator's point of view in the graphic organizer. Use what you learned to discuss point of view in another poem.

Details

Point of View

Respond to Reading

COLLABORATE

Talk about the prompt below. Think about point of view in the poems you read. Use your notes and graphic organizer.

How do the poets of "Empanada Day," "Cold Feet," and "Bugged" help you understand how people figure things out?

_____

_____

_____

_____

_____

_____

_____

_____

_____

_____

_____

Quick Tip

Use these sentence starters to talk about the prompt.

The poem describes …

The narrator wants …

The poets help me visualize events by …

Grammar Connections

As you write your response, make sure to place quotation marks around the title of each poem and any words you copy directly from each poem.

Gathering Information

An interview is a great way to gather information about a person or topic. It is a formal meeting where the interviewer asks a series of questions and writes down the responses.

Jayden: I read that you invented the windshield wipers. How did you get the idea?

Mary Anderson: I was in a streetcar, and the driver kept jumping out to wipe snow off the windshield. I wanted a better way to solve this problem!

What is another question you could ask Mary Anderson?

COLLABORATE

Interview an Inventor Think of an inventor you would like to know more about. Take these steps to write an interview.

1. Research what the person invented and why.
2. Generate a list of three questions.
3. Use your research to write the answers to the questions.
4. Practice reading the interview with your partner. Then, present it to the class.

The Inventor Thinks Up Helicopters

 How does the poet's use of alliteration help you visualize a helicopter?

Literature Anthology: pages 148–149

 Talk About It Reread page 149. Talk with a partner about how the poet's word choice affects the feel of the poem.

Cite Text Evidence How does alliteration help you picture a helicopter? Write text evidence in the chart.

Alliteration	I Visualize

Write The poet's use of alliteration helps me _____

_____

_____

_____

✂ **Combine Information**

Reread "The Inventor Thinks Up Helicopters." Think about the questions the poet asks. How do they help you understand her point of view?

Ornithopter

? **How does the poet use word choice, like onomatopoeia, to help you understand what the flight was like?**

Talk About It Reread page 150. Talk with a partner about how the poet describes the sounds heard during the flight.

Cite Text Evidence What words and phrases describe sounds? Write text evidence in the word web.

Onomatopoeia is the use of a word whose sound suggests its meaning. The word *purr* is an onomatopoeia. It means "a soft, murmuring sound." When you say the word *purr,* it sounds like what it means.

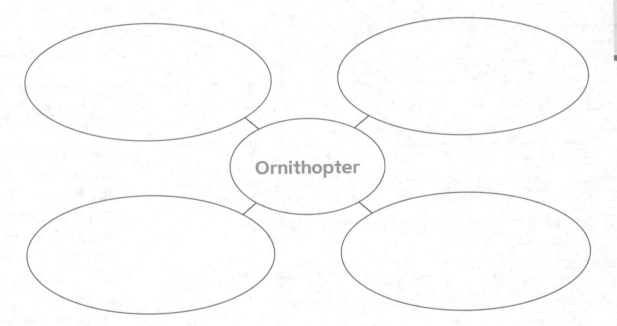

Ornithopter

Write I understand what it was like to be at the flight because

_____

_____

Respond to Reading

Answer the prompt below. Think about how the two poems you read describe inventors. Use your notes and graphic organizer.

How do the poets help you understand how people invent things?

_____

_____

_____

_____

_____

_____

_____

_____

_____

_____

Montgolfier Brothers' Hot Air Balloon

Literature Anthology:
pages 152–153

? How does the poet use the illustration to set the mood for the poem?

Talk About It Look at the illustration on page 152. Talk with a partner about what mood the illustration sets for the poem.

Cite Text Evidence What clues in the illustration help you get a feel for the poem? Write them in the chart.

Make Inferences

Look at colors, details, and facial expressions in illustrations to make an inference about the poem's mood.

Clues	Mood

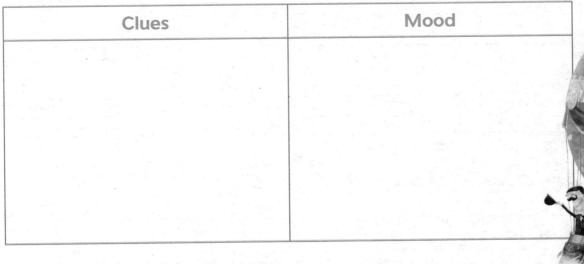

Write The author uses the illustration to set the mood by _____

_____

_____

_____

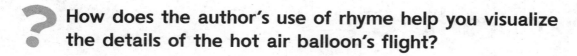

? **How does the author's use of rhyme help you visualize the details of the hot air balloon's flight?**

Quick Tip

I can use these sentence starters when we talk about rhymes:

The rhymes in the poem are . . .

They help me visualize . . .

COLLABORATE

Talk About It Reread the poem on page 153. Talk with a partner about the words that rhyme and how they help you picture the flight.

Cite Text Evidence What rhyming words help you visualize the hot air balloon's flight? Find text evidence and write what you picture.

Montgolfier Brothers' Hot Air Balloon	
Words →	**I Visualize**
→	
→	

Write The author uses rhyme to help me visualize _____

_____

Voice

Poets use language to give their poems a mood or personality. This is called *voice*. Alliteration and rhyme can make the voice of a poem funny, especially when used in unexpected ways. Poets choose words that help readers picture funny actions or events.

 FIND TEXT EVIDENCE

Reread the second stanza of "Montgolfier Brothers' Hot Air Balloon" on page 153 of the **Literature Anthology.** *The poet uses the rhyming words* smart, cart, *and* apart *in the same line. This use of rhyme helps create a humorous tone.*

> Till our smart little cart started falling apart,

 Your Turn Reread "Montgolfier Brothers' Hot Air Balloon" on page 153.

- What unexpected rhyme makes the first stanza feel humorous?

  _____

- What are some other ways the author uses language to create

  a humorous voice? _____

  _____

  _____

Text Connections

? **How do Helen Leah Reed and the poets who wrote the poems you read this week help you understand how people figure things out?**

Talk About It Read "A Curiosity." Talk with a partner about how the boy figures things out.

Cite Text Evidence **Circle** words and phrases in the poem that show the boy is curious. Review the poems you read this week and discuss ways the poets helps you understand how people invent things.

Write Helen Leah Reed and the poets help me understand that people figure

things out by _____

_____

_____

_____

_____

"A Curiosity"

I knew a little boy, not very long ago,
Who was as bright and happy
  as any boy you know.
He had an only fault,
  and you will all agree
That from a fault like this a boy
  himself might free.
"I wonder who is there, oh, see!
  now, why is this?"
And "Oh, where are they going?"
  and "Tell me what it is?"
Ah! "which" and "why"
  and "who," and "what"
  and "where" and "when,"
We often wished that
  never need we
  hear those words again.

       — Helen Leah Reed

Expression and Phrasing

Think about the funny parts of the poems you read. Reading them with **expression** can make poems funnier and more interesting. Knowing when to pause and when to keep reading is called **phrasing**, and it can make poems easier to understand. Punctuation gives clues to a poem's phrasing.

Quick Tip

Poems are often written to be read aloud. Limericks, especially, are meant to be shared aloud. Try to match your tone to the funny tone of the poem as you read.

Page 166

Our washing machine is a bear
That munches up socks by the pair.
He will suds them and grumble
As they spin, turn, and tumble,
Then spit them out, ready to wear.

When a line doesn't end in punctuation, you can read on to the next line more quickly.

A comma in the middle of a line shows that you should make a slight pause as you read.

Your Turn Look at page 167. Take turns reading "Bugged" aloud with a partner. Pay attention to punctuation. Listen to how the alliteration and rhyme build a rhythm. Try to express the poet's feelings as you read the poem.

Think about how you did. Complete these sentences.

I remembered to _____

_____

Next time I will _____

_____

Literature Anthology:
pages 148-149

Expert Model

Features of Poetry

Poetry is different from other forms of writing. It's a form that focuses on experiences, feelings, and ideas. A free verse poem

- can have any number of lines and stanzas, which are grouped sets of lines

- does not always rhyme

- uses alliteration, onomatopoeia, and other types of figurative language that appeals to the readers' senses

Analyze an Expert Model Reread "The Inventor Thinks Up Helicopters" on page 149 in the **Literature Anthology**. Use text evidence to answer the questions below.

How does the poet use figurative language?

_____

_____

How does the poet's use of both long and short lines help to describe the movement of a helicopter?

_____

_____

Word Wise

On page 149, poet Patricia Hubbell uses onomatopoeia to make her poem appeal to your senses. The word *whirling* means quickly turning. When you say *whirling,* it sounds like what it means.

Plan: Choose Your Topic

COLLABORATE

Brainstorm With a partner, think about a time that you had to figure something out. Talk about a plan or invention and how it could solve a problem. Use these sentence starters:

The problem is . . .

A fun invention that would solve the problem is . . .

This invention would . . .

Writing Prompt Choose one of the plans or inventions to write a free verse poem about.

I will write about _____

Purpose and Audience An author's purpose is the main reason for writing. Your audience is who will be reading your poem.

The reason I chose this topic is _____

_____

I want my audience to feel _____

_____

Freewrite In your writer's notebook, write as many ideas as you can think of about your invention. What problem does it solve? How did you think of it? What is most important about it? Write as many words as you can that will help you describe it.

Plan: Ideas

Ideas Poets use interesting words and details to bring their ideas to life and help readers paint a mental picture of what is being described in the poem.

Let's look at another expert model. Reread these lines from "Empanada Day."

> One bite of Abuelita's empanadas
>
> And my mouth purrs like a cat.

The word *purrs* is an onomatopoeia, or a word that sounds like what it means. How does it help you understand how the narrator feels about empanadas?

_____

_____

_____

 Plan In your writer's notebook, draw a Word Web. Write the topic of your free verse poem in the middle oval. Then write words that describe your ideas.

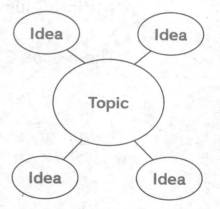

Draft

Rhythm and Rhyme Poets use rhyme schemes, or patterns, to make poems sound musical. A free verse poem might not rhyme, but it has a rhythm, or pattern formed by stressed syllables.

These two lines from "Empanada Day" rhyme. They also have the same rhythm. You can hear it by reading the lines aloud.

> "Teach me," I beg and bounce on my feet,
>
> "Teach me to make this magical treat."

Now use these first two lines as a model to write about how you figured something out. Use rhyming words and rhythm.

_____

_____

_____

Write a Draft Use your Word Web to write your draft in your writer's notebook. Choose words that make your poem musical and your ideas come to life.

Quick Tip

Remember that a draft is just your first time writing. Don't worry about making everything perfect. You will have time to fix any mistakes later. Just try to get all your ideas written down.

Revise

Figurative Language Poets use figurative language, such as similes and onomatopoeia. A simile compares two different things. Onomatopoeia describes words that sound like what they mean. Both help readers form pictures in their minds.

Read the poem below. Think about words and phrases you can add to make it more interesting to read. Then revise the poem by adding figurative language.

My sneakers take me all over town,

We go up and down hills, jump across puddles.

I've had these sneakers a very long time.

_____

_____

_____

_____

 Revise Revise your draft. Make sure you choose words that help readers picture your ideas.

Peer Conferences

Review a Draft Listen carefully as your partner reads his or her draft aloud. Say what you like about the draft. Use these sentence starters to discuss your partner's draft.

I like this part of the poem because I could see . . .

Can you use rhyme or rhythm here to . . .

Use more figurative language to help me picture . . .

Partner Feedback After you take turns giving each other feedback, write one of the suggestions from your partner that you will use in your revision.

_____

_____

_____

_____

_____

Revision After you finish your peer conference, use the Revising Checklist to figure out what you can change to make your poem better. Remember to use the rubric on page 191.

Revising Checklist

☐ Are my ideas clearly described?

☐ Did I use figurative language?

☐ Is there rhyme and/ or rhythm in my poem?

☐ Did I choose words that are funny and memorable?

Tech Tip

Word processing programs will give you the choice of using different fonts, or letter styles. This useful tool can make your writing more descriptive and interesting to read.

Edit and Proofread

When you edit and proofread your writing, you look for and correct mistakes in grammar, spelling, and punctuation. Read your draft at least three times. This will help you catch any mistakes. Use the checklist below to edit your poem.

✔ Editing Checklist

☐ Do all lines begin with a capital letter?

☐ Is there punctuation at the end of every sentence?

☐ Are there apostrophes in possessive nouns?

☐ Are all words spelled correctly?

List two mistakes that you found as you proofread your poem.

1 _____

_____

_____

2 _____

_____

_____

Grammar Connections

When you proofread your draft for punctuation mistakes, remember to use an apostrophe to show possession. For example, "My sister's sneakers are bright blue."

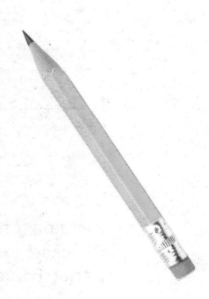

Publish, Present, and Evaluate

Publishing When you publish your writing, you create a neat final copy that is free of mistakes. If you are not using a computer, use your best handwriting. Write legibly in print or cursive.

Presentation When you are ready to present, practice your presentation. Use the presenting checklist.

Evaluate After you publish, use the rubric to evaluate your poem.

What did you do successfully? _____

_____

What needs more work? _____

_____

Presenting Checklist

☐ Look at your audience.

☐ Speak loudly and clearly.

☐ Use expression to convey the mood of your poem.

☐ Pause at the end of lines or phrases.

4	3	2	1
• excellent use of figurative language; descriptions are vivid • excellent use of rhyme and rhythm; writing is smooth and fun to read • includes correct spelling and grammar	• good use of figurative language; descriptions are clear • good use of rhyme and rhythm; writing sounds like poetry • has a spelling or grammar error	• some use of figurative language; descriptions are somewhat unclear • some use of rhyme and rhythm; writing is choppy in places • has several spelling or grammar errors	• no use of figurative language; descriptions are unclear • no use of rhyme and rhythm; writing is difficult to understand • has frequent spelling or grammar errors

Spiral Review

You have learned new skills and strategies in Unit 2 that will help you read more critically. Now it is time to practice what you have learned.

- **Prefixes**
- **Headings**
- **Reread**
- **Author's Point of View**
- **Make Predictions**
- **Theme**
- **Point of View**
- **Similes**

Connect to Content

- **Create a Venn Diagram**
- **Write a Public Service Announcement**
- **Reading Digitally**

Read the selection and choose the best answer to each question.

Solving Local PROBLEMS

1   If you have a problem at home, you ask an adult for help. If you have a problem at school, you ask your teacher for help. But what if you have a problem in your community? Whom would you turn to for help?

Local Leaders

2   Local governments take care of issues in cities or towns. A state's constitution often determines how local governments are set up.

3   In many cities and towns, a mayor is the leader of the local government. The people elect their mayor by voting. Other cities and towns might have a city manager. A city manager is not elected, but instead is appointed by the state government.

4   Mayors do not work alone. There is usually a group of people, called a city council, who work with the mayor. Together they make important decisions and solve problems. The members of the city council are elected by people.

The mayor and city council members work together with police officers, firefighters, and park managers.

Solving Problems

5   Local governments deal with many kinds of public issues. They deal with anything from street signs and roads, to parks and schools, to trash and sewers.

6   When citizens have a concern in their community, they can go to their local government. For example, someone might want a stop sign put on a corner near her home. She might think that people drive too fast. Or a person might want his street repaved, because it has big holes.

7   There are many ways to tell your local government about a problem. City councils hold meetings that are open to citizens. They can attend to listen and voice concerns. The mayor and city council then look into problems and reach a solution. Citizens can also write letters to their government. And many local governments have websites where citizens can get information and contact the mayor or city council.

8   Local governments are a great resource for citizens. Find out who is part of your local government. That way, if you have a problem, you'll know whom to contact.

©Hill Street Studios/Blend Images LLC

SHOW WHAT YOU LEARNED

1 What information can you find under the section heading "Solving Problems"?

Para 6

A how a mayor of a city or town is elected

B ways to contact your local government

C the definition of a city council

D who determines the functions of a local government

Quick Tip

Rereading can help you with words and sentences you might not understand the first time you read a passage. This helps you understand the topic better.

2 What is the author's point of view about local governments?

Para 8

F They are made up of a mayor and city council.

G They are a great resource for citizens.

H They solve citizens' problems.

J They deal with many kinds of issues.

3 In paragraph 6, what does the word repaved mean?

A paved again

B not paved

C paved before

D paved after

4 Reread paragraph 7. Which is NOT a way the author includes to contact a local government?

F visiting the website

G writing a letter

H calling by phone

J attending a meeting

Read the selection and choose the best answer to each question.

★ WELCOME TO ★
AMERICA

1   Shannon tried to keep up with her older brother, but he always walked too fast. Ma had told them to walk together, because she didn't trust the streets of New York.

2   When Shannon finally caught up to him, he was talking to a girl she had never seen before. She was sitting on the stoop of their apartment building, her hair as red as the bricks behind her.

3   "What's your name?" Patrick was practically shouting at the girl, who looked confused and scared.

4   "Why are you yelling?" Shannon asked.

5   "I'm not yelling," Patrick replied. "I don't think she understands English."

6   "Shouting isn't going to help her understand," Shannon said. Then she turned to the girl and said, "Hi, my name is Shannon."

7   The girl stared at Shannon, and then ran as quickly as a mouse inside the building. Patrick and Shannon followed after her, but she disappeared behind a first-floor door.

8   Just then, Ma was coming down the stairs. "Her family just arrived here from Ireland," Ma explained. "She doesn't speak English, just Irish."

9   Shannon and Patrick wanted to help the girl feel at home in America. Their father had told them stories about when he had moved from Ireland to America. He didn't know English, and he had to learn it by himself. Shannon and Patrick decided they would help the new girl learn English so she wouldn't be so scared.

10   After supper, Patrick showed Shannon a book he'd found on the bookcase. It was a dictionary that listed words in Irish and English. "Let's learn Irish words so we can talk to the new girl," he said.

11   With the dictionary and Ma's and Da's help, the two learned simple Irish words and phrases.

12   The next morning, Shannon and Patrick started walking to school. Just ahead of them was the red-haired girl. Shannon and Patrick walked faster to catch up to her.

13   She looked scared again until Shannon said hello in Irish. Then Patrick asked, in Irish, "What is your name?"

14   The red-haired girl stopped, smiled, and said, "Orla."

15   Shannon and Patrick smiled too and said, "Welcome to America, Orla!"

1 Why did Orla run away from Patrick and Shannon?

   A She was scared and confused.

   B She wanted them to chase her.

   C She thought Patrick was being a bully.

   D She needed to get home for supper.

2 In paragraph 2, the author uses a simile to describe —

   F Shannon's feelings

   G Patrick's voice

   H The apartment building

   J Orla's hair

3 Which statement describes a main theme of the story?

   A It is not wise to talk to strangers.

   B It is important to overcome your fears.

   C It is good to help new people feel welcome.

   D It is smart to turn to books when you do not know something.

4 Based on information in the story, what will most likely happen next?

   F Orla will make a lot of new friends.

   G Orla will learn to speak English.

   H Orla's family will move back to Ireland.

   J Orla will not be happy in America.

Quick Tip

When you make predictions, use what you know about the characters and your own experiences to decide what might happen next.

COMPARING GENRES

COLLABORATE

- In the **Literature Anthology,** reread the historical fiction passage *The Castle on Hester Street* on pages 126–141 and the free verse poem "The Inventor Thinks Up Helicopters" on page 149.

- Use the Venn Diagram below to show how the two genres are the alike and different.

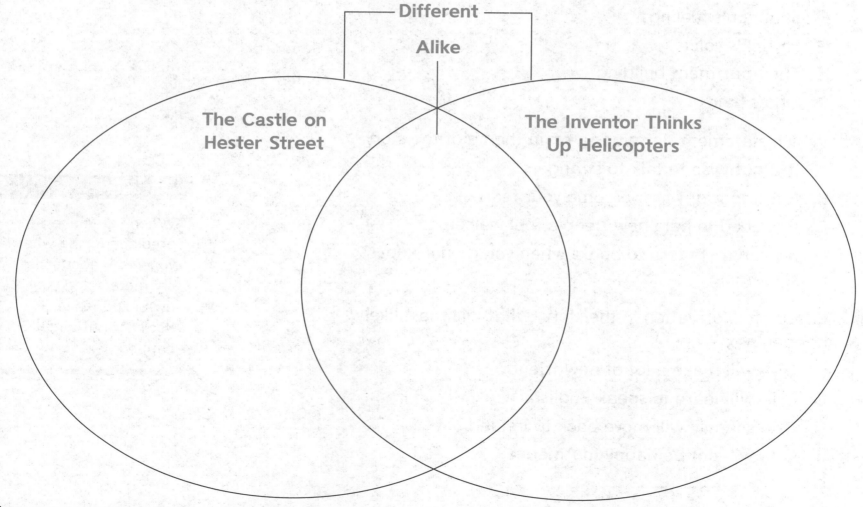

Different

Alike

The Castle on Hester Street

The Inventor Thinks Up Helicopters

HOMOGRAPHS

Homographs are words that are spelled the same but have different meanings. They are sometimes pronounced differently. Use nearby words as clues to help you figure out the meaning of a homograph. You can also check the meanings of homographs in a classroom or online dictionary.

Read these sentences. The word *post* is a homograph. Talk with a partner about its different meanings.

I took a photograph of the bird's nest on the fence **post** in front of my house. Now I plan to **post** it on my blog about birds.

Write what the word *post* means in each sentence:

Definition 1: _____

_____

_____

Definition 2: _____

_____

_____

Blend Images/Image Source

CREATE A VENN DIAGRAM

A Venn diagram shows how two things are alike and different.

• Research two services your local government provides.

• Think about how the two services are alike and different.

• Create a Venn diagram like the one on page 198 to show how the services are alike and different.

I chose these two services because _____

The biggest difference between the two services is

_____

WRITE A PUBLIC SERVICE ANNOUNCEMENT

A public service announcement informs people about an issue. Write a public service announcement to convince others to help new students at your school.

• Grab your audience's attention.

• Use words to persuade your audience to act.

• Make your announcement short and to the point.

Something I learned while writing my public service

announcement is _____

A HUNT TO HELP FROGS

Online articles have text features, like print articles. They also have interactive features. Read the online article "A Hunt to Help Frogs." Find two interactive features within the text. Write what they are below. Log on to **my.mheducation.com**

A Hunt to Help Frogs

Scientists search for long-lost frogs, salamanders, and toads.

Time for Kids: "A Hunt to Help Frogs"

 1 _____

 2 _____

Read the article all the way through. Then reread it and click on the interactive features in the right column. Write your answers to the questions below.

- Look at the interactive map, "Lost and Found Frogs and Toads." Name three frogs that have been found.

_____

- According to the author, why are frogs important?

_____

_____

- Reread the section "Frogs in Danger." Name four reasons that frog populations are shrinking.

_____

_____

TRACK YOUR PROGRESS

WHAT DID YOU LEARN?

Use the rubric to evaluate yourself on the skills that you learned in this unit. Write your scores in the boxes below.

4	3	2	1
I can successfully identify all examples of this skill.	I can identify most examples of this skill.	I can identify a few examples of this skill.	I need to work on this skill more.

☐ Author's Point of View   ☐ Theme   ☐ Point of View

☐ Prefixes   ☐ Similes   ☐ Homographs

Something I need to work more on is _____ because

_____

_____

_____

Text-to-Self Think back over the texts that you have read in this unit. Choose one text and write a short paragraph explaining a personal connection that you have made to the text.

I made a personal connection to _____

because _____

_____

Present Your Work

Decide how you will present your interview with an inventor. Use the presenting checklist as you practice your presentation. Discuss the sentence starters below and write your answers.

An interesting fact I learned about my inventor is

_____

_____

I would like to know more about

_____

One more question I would ask is

_____

I think my presentation was

_____

Quick Tip

Use a mirror to practice looking up at your audience. Also practice using two voices, one for the interviewer asking the questions and one for the person answering.

Presenting Checklist

☐ I will practice reading my interview out loud.

☐ I will read facts clearly.

☐ I will speak loudly enough for all to hear.

☐ I will use my voice to express the two people in the interview.